HAPPINESS AND GOODNESS

HAPPINESS

and GOODNESS

Philosophical
Reflections on
Living Well

STEVEN M. CAHN
CHRISTINE VITRANO

Columbia University Press   *New York*

Columbia University Press
Publishers Since 1893
New York   Chichester, West Sussex
cup.columbia.edu
Copyright © 2015 Columbia University Press
All rights reserved

Library of Congress Cataloging-in-Publication Data
Cahn, Steven M.
Happiness and goodness : philosophical reflections on living well /
Steven M. Cahn and Christine Vitrano.
pages cm
Includes bibliographical references and index.
ISBN 978-0-231-17240-0 (cloth : alk. paper) —
ISBN 978-0-231-17241-7 (pbk. : alk. paper) —
ISBN 978-0-231-53936-4 (e-book)
1. Life. 2. Conduct of life. 3. Happiness. 4. Well-being. I. Title.

BD431.C224 2015
171'.3—dc23
2014041694

∞

Columbia University Press books are printed on
permanent and durable acid-free paper.
This book is printed on paper with recycled content.
Printed in the United States of America

c 10 9 8 7 6 5 4 3 2 1
p 10 9 8 7 6 5 4 3 2 1

Cover and book design: Lisa Hamm

References to websites (URLs) were accurate at the time
of writing. Neither the author nor Columbia University Press
is responsible for URLs that may have expired or changed
since the manuscript was prepared.

CONTENTS

FUTILITY
86

LIVING WELL
90

23

SATISFACTION
94

24

CONCLUDING QUESTIONS
97

FOREWORD

Robert B. Talisse

PROFESSOR: Why have you enrolled in my course?

STUDENT: Because it's required for my major.

PROFESSOR: But why are you doing what's required for your major?

STUDENT: Because I want to complete my degree.

PROFESSOR: But why do you want to complete your degree?

STUDENT: Because I want to get a good job.

PROFESSOR: But why do you want to get a good job?

STUDENT: Because I want to earn a good salary.

PROFESSOR: But why do you want to earn a good salary?

STUDENT: So that I can afford to buy the things I want—a nice house, a fast car, delicious food, fashionable clothes, and so on.

PROFESSOR: But why do you want those things?

STUDENT: Because having them will make me happy.

PROFESSOR: But why do you want to be happy?

STUDENT: Huh?

It was probably Aristotle who first took note of the special role that the concept of happiness plays in our thinking about how to live. Happiness, he argued, is the final end of all human activity, that for the sake of which every action is performed. The Student is perplexed at the end of the exchange above because the Professor, in posing her final question, betrays a lack of familiarity with this basic Aristotelian insight. The Student understands that there really is no response to the question "Why do you want to be happy?" To identify an action as necessary for one's happiness is to explain why one would even perform it. When explaining human action, happiness is where the buck stops.

Aristotle's insight seems undeniable and, understandably, it remains popular among philosophers. However, like most undeniable philosophical claims, it ultimately does not tell us much. To identify happiness as the definitive aim of human action is to simply assert that we do what we think will bring us happiness. It is to say that when we act, we act for the sake of *what we take to be* happiness. As appearances can be deceiving, deep questions persist about what happiness is.

Perhaps this is why Aristotle affirmed further that happiness is the culmination of all of the good things a human life could manifest. He claimed that the truly happy person not only derives great enjoyment from living, but is also both morally and cognitively flawless. In fact, Aristotle goes so far as to posit that the happy person necessarily has friends, good looks, health, and wealth. And, as if these advantages were not enough, he holds that the fully happy person is invulnerable even to misfortune and bad luck. According to Aristotle, then, happiness is not simply that for the sake of which we act; it is that which renders a human life complete, lacking nothing that could improve it.

Few philosophers today subscribe to Aristotle's view that complete success in every evaluative dimension is strictly required for happiness. Most will readily concede that a person could be happy and yet not especially intelligent, beautiful, or wealthy; some even argue that a happy life typically involves various kinds of deficiency. Still, a slightly more modest version of Aristotle's second claim continues to be influential among contemporary moral philosophers.

This is the idea that the immoral person is necessarily unhappy, that morality is necessary for happiness.

The attraction of this view is easy to discern. Since Plato, moral philosophers have been embroiled in a confrontation with immoralism, which is the view that morality is some kind of sham. The immoralist's challenge is often posed as a simple question: "Why be moral?" In asking this, the immoralist demands an account of why one should be *motivated* to act according to morality's demands, especially given that to do so is often burdensome. Interestingly, most versions of immoralism accept Aristotle's initial claim that happiness is the ultimate aim of human action, and they typically accept the further thought that happiness renders one's life successful as well. What the immoralist denies, then, is that anyone has a good reason to be moral. However, if it could be shown that being moral is necessary for happiness, then immoralism would be defeated. The moralist's argument against immoralism looks simple enough: One aims ultimately to be happy, and morality is necessary for happiness; therefore, one has sufficient reason to be moral. Again, the buck stops with happiness.

Contemporary moral philosophers tend to presuppose the success of some version of this simple argument. Believing they have settled the matter of why one should be moral, philosophers have almost exclusively attended to the task of discerning morality's requirements. The results have been impressive. We now have highly developed versions of almost every conceivable theory of morality, and the long-running academic debates among those who propose competing views is fascinating. But in recent years some have expressed frustration with the technicalities of moral philosophy; they have aspired to reconnect the discipline to the larger questions of morality's relation to happiness and living well.

This broadening of moral philosophy's scope is well timed. Academic interest with happiness is widespread and growing. Researchers from fields as diverse as psychology, economics, history, art, medicine, theology, business, and biology have taken up research about happiness. At present, there is not only a *Journal of*

Happiness Studies, a *Journal of Happiness and Well-Being*, and a *Journal of Happiness and Development*, but also many scholarly societies and research institutes devoted to inquiry regarding happiness, well-being, and related phenomena worldwide. In 2012, the United Nations General Assembly declared March 20th the "International Day of Happiness."

Perhaps more importantly, contemporary popular culture seems obsessed with happiness. Given this, happiness is a big business. Effective speakers on the topic are able to command handsome fees for giving speeches to corporate and popular audiences. In Hollywood and elsewhere, it is possible to earn a quite comfortable salary as a "life coach" or a "spiritual adviser" to wealthy and powerful clients. Talk-show personalities and made-for-television psychologists appear daily to advise their viewers on all matters pertaining to happiness, spirituality, and emotional well-being. Even the tiniest chain bookstores in Nashville, Tennessee, stock dozens of titles promising to help a popular readership achieve happiness.

Judging from these various materials, happiness is shrouded in mystery. A casual glance at my bookseller's shelves suggests that there are "secrets" to happiness that must be "uncovered," "unlocked," "embraced," "affirmed," and "energized." A slightly less casual investigation reveals that the more ambitious Aristotelian claim still thrives; in the popular views, happiness is understood to encompass all of life's goods, including beauty, health, love, influence, popularity, and, of course, money. All of this makes for good marketing. Were happiness something obvious or easy, there would be no need for all of the books, lectures, and gurus. Yet one needn't examine these materials too closely to find suggestions of debatable value. According to some, the way to achieve happiness—and all of its varied goods—is to recite the right words at the beginning of each day; others claim the key is eating the right foods; some recommend meditation; others prescribe physical exercise and plenty of sleep; some recommend elaborate psychological rituals to keep one focused on one's goals; others claim that happiness is mainly a matter of keeping one's household possessions neatly organized.

The variety is truly staggering. To put a cynical gloss on these matters, a lot of people are making a fortune selling dubious advice about how to be happy.

Against this complex academic and cultural backdrop, Steven M. Cahn and Christine Vitrano offer *Happiness and Goodness*, their "philosophical reflections on living well." The direct and often playful tone of this text should not be mistaken for simplemindedness or naiveté. Their critical maneuvers often cut deeply, and their positive view is a formidable one. Their central thesis can be put succinctly: Morality is not necessary for happiness. The immoral person might be a completely happy person, and the moral saint might nonetheless be absolutely miserable.

Of course, with morality and happiness decoupled, the immoralist challenge reemerges. Why be moral then? Yet Cahn and Vitrano do not endorse the immoralist conclusion that no one has reason to be moral. Although they do register a few serious concerns about the most popular theories of morality, they are not moral skeptics. They argue only that morality requires a grounding that is independent of human happiness. With its claim that living well is simply a matter of achieving happiness within the bounds of morality, the positive project of Cahn and Vitrano's book is to devise a conception of happiness compatible with any plausible theory of morality.

As the authors duly recognize, their account of happiness draws heavily from the Epicurean tradition, supplemented with important insights from the Biblical text Ecclesiastes (known in Hebrew as *Koheleth*). The core of their view is that happiness is neither mysterious nor particularly difficult to achieve. It does not require a love of truth or an overriding desire to avoid ignorance and illusion; nor is it reserved only for those who engage in lofty intellectual pursuits, such as philosophy. To be happy, they say, is to engage in those activities that one finds to be particularly enjoyable, whatever they may be. Of course, the pursuit of this enjoyment must be guided by prudence. Living well, then, is pursuing enjoyment prudently and within the bounds of morality.

I leave it to the reader to weigh the merits of Cahn and Vitrano's argument. Surely this assessment should involve a comparison of the authors' position with other competing accounts. It should be said that one of the especially refreshing aspects of this intriguing little book is the authors' discussion of some of the other views in currency. To be frank, I was surprised to find that so many contemporary philosophers have seen fit to identify some activities as intrinsically hollow and thus not conducive to happiness. Cahn and Vitrano do a nice job of exposing the folly in this. One can only wonder why academic philosophers might take themselves to be so equipped to pronounce on the relative merits of lives devoted to such things as raising pigs, mastering checkers, completing crosswords, and playing computer games. Why exactly might a philosopher declare these activities vacuous, wasteful, or devoid of meaning?

The answer, I think, is that contemporary moral philosophers are still rather attracted to the more ambitious Aristotelian claim discussed above. Their official denials notwithstanding, many philosophers are inclined to think that happiness must involve success along all evaluative dimensions, a life lacking nothing that could improve it. These philosophers are thus disposed to regard a life focused on seemingly trivial pursuits to be squandered, hampered, deficient, and therefore unhappy. Yet, as Cahn and Vitrano argue, just as one must admit the possibility of a happy immoralist, one must also admit that lives that appear mundane, trifling, and pointless to academic philosophers can nonetheless be filled with happiness.

I suspect that, in the end, many professional ethicists who are interested in the theory of happiness will be unmoved by the arguments found in this text. They will endeavor to defend the idea that happiness is elusive, complicated, difficult to achieve, and hence rare. No doubt many will continue to regard happiness as requiring not only moral behavior, but also the pursuit of lofty goals and high-minded objectives. The determination among academic philosophers to support conceptions of happiness that in effect condemn most people to lives of inescapable despondency is difficult to understand. But, thankfully, this provocative book, with its unusual combination of sharp debates, compelling examples, and insightful humor, presents a serious challenge to the current philosophical orthodoxy.

* * *

Robert B. Talisse is professor of philosophy and political science and chair of the Philosophy Department at Vanderbilt University.

PREFACE

This work draws in part on our published books and articles, including those we authored individually or jointly. All the material, however, has been reworked to provide a unified presentation of a position we have developed over many years.

Here are our sources:

Cahn, Steven M. *A New Introduction to Philosophy.* New York: Harper & Row, 1971. Reprinted in 2004 by Wipf & Stock Publishers.

——. *Education and the Democratic Ideal.* Chicago: Nelson-Hall, 1979. Reprinted in 2004 by Wipf & Stock Publishers.

——. *God, Reason, and Religion.* Belmont, Calif.: Thomson/Wadworth, 2006.

——. *Puzzles & Perplexities.* 2nd edition. Lanham, Md: Lexington Books, 2007.

Vitrano, Christine. *The Nature and Value of Happiness.* Boulder, Colo.: Westview Press, 2014.

——. "The Happy Immoralist." In *A Teacher's Life: Essays for Steven M. Cahn,* edited by Robert B. Talisse and Maureen Eckert, 149–53. Lanham, Md.: Lexington Books, 2009.

———. "The Subjectivity of Happiness." *Journal of Value Inquiry* 44, no. 1 (2010): 47–54.

———. "Meaningful Lives." *Ratio* 26, no. 1 (2013): 79–90.

———. "Meaningful Lives?" In *Exploring Ethics*, edited by Steven M. Cahn, 462–64. 3rd ed. New York: Oxford University Press, 2014.

Cahn, Steven M., and Christine Vitrano. *Happiness: Classic and Contemporary Readings in Philosophy*. New York: Oxford University Press, 2008.

———. "Choosing the Experience Machine." *Philosophy in the Contemporary World* 20, no. 1 (2013): 52–58.

———. "Living Well." *Think* 13 (Autumn 2014): 13–23.

✱ ✱ ✱

We wish to express appreciation to Wendy Lochner, our editor at Columbia University Press, for her support and guidance. We also wish to thank assistant editor Christine Dunbar, manuscript editor Kathryn Jorge, and other members of the staff of the Press for their generous help.

We are especially grateful to Robert B. Talisse for his illuminating foreword, and deeply appreciate his kind words.

HAPPINESS AND GOODNESS

1

INTRODUCTION

How do we assess a person's life? Do we ask how successful the person was in terms of fame, achievement, acquisitions, or relationships? Do we consider what major problems that person faced with health, family, career, or society?

Yet even after these questions are answered, other fundamental ones remain: Was the person happy? Did the person treat others ethically? Did the person live well?

Many philosophers suppose that answers to this second set of questions depend on answers to the first. Our view, however, is that the two sets are independent. In other words, morality, happiness, and quality of life do not follow from activities, accomplishments, or acclaim.

Note that we do not defend a specific moral theory. Instead, we assume that any moral person cares about others, treats them with respect, and seeks to minimize their suffering. Further complications abound, but these are not our focus.

Nor do we distinguish various terms that indicate that a person's whole life should be viewed positively. Thus we treat as synonymous "achieving well-being," "attaining meaning," and "living well," although most often we refer to the last.

Instead, we ask what are the connections between morality, happiness, and living well? Our answer is that moral behavior is not necessary for happiness and does not ensure it. Morality and happiness, however, are needed for living well, and together suffice to achieve that goal.

We shall explain this view and defend it against arguments of those contemporary philosophers who disagree with us. We include historical references, but unlike many others who have written on these topics, we do not present our ideas as commentary on the writings of Plato or Aristotle. We do, however, link our position to elements within both the Hellenistic and Hebraic traditions.

We begin by considering reflections on the good life offered by the late political and legal theorist Ronald Dworkin. Although we do not find his conclusions persuasive, his presentation offers a convenient gateway to discussion of our main subject.

2

WASTED LIVES?

I n Dworkin's posthumously published *Religion Without God*, he argues that an atheist can be religious. While this claim would come as no surprise to adherents of Jainism, Theravada Buddhism, or Mimamsa Hinduism, he has in mind not these Asian religious traditions but a viewpoint common to many Western thinkers who deny theism yet recognize "nature's intrinsic beauty" and the "inescapable responsibility" of people to "live their lives well."[1] Dworkin considers such an outlook religious.

Leaving aside his curious line of thought that finds support for religious belief in such disparate phenomena as the Grand Canyon, prowling jaguars, and the discovery by physicists of the Higgs boson, let us concentrate on his view that we should all seek to live well so as to achieve "successful" lives and avoid "wasted" ones.[2]

Does one model fit all? On this important point Dworkin wavers. He maintains that "there is, independently and objectively, a right way to live." Yet he also recognizes "a responsibility of each person to decide for himself ethical questions about which kinds of lives are appropriate and which would be degrading for him."[3]

What sort of life did Dworkin himself find degrading? We are not told but suspect that for such a successful academic, a "degrading life" might have been one without intellectual striving, just as a famed athlete might find degrading life as a couch potato.

But of all possible lives, which are well-lived? To help answer this question, consider the following two fictional, though realistic, cases.

Pat received a bachelor's degree from a prestigious college and a Ph.D. in philosophy from a leading university, then was awarded an academic position at a first-rate school, and eventually earned tenure there. Pat is the author of numerous books, articles, and reviews, is widely regarded as a leading scholar and teacher, and is admired by colleagues and students for fairness and helpfulness. Pat is happily married, has two children, enjoys playing bridge and the cello, and vacations each summer in a modest house on Cape Cod. Physically and mentally healthy, Pat is in good spirits, looking forward to years of happiness.

Lee, on the other hand, did not attend college. After high school Lee moved to a beach community in California and is devoted to sunbathing, swimming, and surfing. Lee has never married but has experienced numerous romances. Having inherited wealth from deceased parents, Lee has no financial needs but, while donating generously to worthy causes, spends money freely on magnificent homes, luxury cars, designer clothes, fine dining, golfing holidays, and extensive travel. Lee has many friends and is admired for honesty and kindness. Physically and mentally healthy, Lee is in good spirits, looking forward to years of happiness.

Both Pat and Lee live in ways that appear to suit them. Both enjoy prosperity, treat others with respect, engage in activities they find fulfilling, and report they are happy. Are both living equally well? In other words, are both pursuing equally meaningful lives? Or, alternatively, is either life wasted?

Dworkin offers little guidance to help answer these questions. He urges that we make our lives into works of art,[4] but works of art typically contain complexities and conflicts not found in the lives of Pat or Lee. The story of each might be told in the form of a play or novel, but neither individual appears to have the makings of Medea, Hamlet, or Anna Karenina.

Dworkin also remarks that "someone creates a work of art from his life if he lives and loves well in family or community with no fame or artistic achievement at all."[5] Here Dworkin, having urged us to live well by making our lives into works of art, unhelpfully suggests that works of art are those made by living well. This circular explanation sheds no light on how to live well, so Dworkin's appeal to works of art does not help us choose between the lives of Pat and Lee.

Many other philosophers, however, have provided reasons for believing that Pat's life is superior to Lee's. These thinkers rate the pursuit of philosophical inquiry, playing the cello, or raising a family, more highly than surfing, a series of romances, or a luxurious home.

Yet not all philosophers agree with this assessment. Two who do not are Richard Taylor and Harry Frankfurt, each of whom would maintain that Pat and Lee are living equally well.

Consider first Taylor's approach. He discusses the case of Sisyphus, who, according to Greek myth, was condemned for his misdeeds to the eternal task of rolling a huge stone to the top of a hill, only each time to have it roll down to the bottom again. Is the activity of Sisyphus meaningless? Taylor concludes that the answer depends on whether Sisyphus has a desire to roll stones up hills. Most of us don't, but if Sisyphus does, then he has found "mission and meaning."[6] Therefore, according to Taylor, living well is living in accord with your desires. If your activities match your wishes, then your life is successful. Whether the activity is teaching philosophy, driving luxury cars, or rolling stones up hills makes no difference.

Frankfurt reaches a similar conclusion. He maintains that we infuse our lives with meaning by loving certain intrinsic ends and caring about the means to achieve them. Need the ends themselves be of a particular sort? Not according to Frankfurt. As he writes, "Devoting oneself to what one loves suffices to make one's life meaningful, regardless of the inherent or objective character of the objects that are loved."[7] Because Pat loves discussing philosophy, playing bridge, and spending time with family, while Lee loves surfing, golfing, and engaging in romantic adventures, both, according to Frankfurt, possess the essentials of a meaningful life.

As we noted, however, most philosophers reject this view of what makes a life significant.[8] They maintain that certain activities are more worthy than others, so lives spent engaged in those more worthy activities are more worthy lives. But which activities have more worth and which less? And on what bases should we decide such matters?

We shall next consider in turn three much-discussed attempts to provide persuasive answers to these questions.

3

PROJECTS OF WORTH?

Susan Wolf maintains that "meaningful lives are lives of active engagement in projects of worth." To be actively engaged is to be "gripped, excited, involved."[1] As for "projects of worth," they are those that are "worthwhile," a term Wolf recognizes as suggesting "a commitment to some sort of objective value," while admitting that she has "neither a philosophical theory of what objective value is nor a substantive theory about what has this sort of value."[2]

She does, however, offer numerous examples of activities she believes are sources of meaning and ones that are not. Among those that yield meaning are moral or intellectual accomplishments, relationships with friends and relatives, aesthetic enterprises, religious practices, climbing a mountain, training for a marathon, campaigning for a political candidate, caring for an ailing friend, and developing one's powers as a cellist, cabinetmaker, or pastry chef.[3]

Among those that do not yield meaning are collecting rubber bands, memorizing the dictionary, making handwritten copies of *War and Peace*, riding a roller coaster, meeting a movie star, finding a great dress on sale, loving a pet goldfish, lying on the beach on a beautiful day, eating a perfectly ripe peach, watching sitcoms, recycling, playing computer games, solving cross-word puzzles, and writing checks to Oxfam and the ACLU. Wolf warns especially against "focusing too narrowly on the superficial goals of ease, prestige, and material wealth."[4]

Controversial cases for her include a life single-mindedly given to corporate law, one devoted to a religious cult, and, an example she takes from David Wiggins, a pig farmer who buys more land to grow more corn to feed more pigs to buy more land to grow more corn to feed more pigs.[5]

Individuals she cites as paradigms of having had meaningful lives are Mother Theresa, Einstein, Cézanne, and "Gandhi, per-haps." Among those she mentions whose lives may lack meaning are "the alienated housewife, the conscripted soldier, the assembly line worker."[6]

These lists, unfortunately, raise more questions than they answer. Why are involvements with religious practices clearly meaningful but not devotion to a religious cult? Why is caring for an ailing friend meaningful but not providing support for a sick stranger? Why is solving crossword puzzles not an intellectual accomplish-ment? Why is meeting a movie star meaningless? Does Wolf sup-pose meeting a famous philosopher would be more meaningful? Why is having met David Lewis more meaningful than having met W. C. Fields?

Why is single-minded concentration on corporate law a con-troversial case? Would single-minded concentration on labor law, patent law, or constitutional law also be controversial? Does single-minded concentration on epistemology escape controversy?

Why is developing one's powers as a pastry chef meaningful, but eating a peach is not? If we can find meaning by preparing food, why can't we find meaning by eating it? Why is meaning found in cam-paigning for a political candidate who is an advocate of the ACLU, yet not found in providing funds to support the activities of the ACLU?

Why is meaning absent if one is drafted and then fights to defend one's country? Is the problem supposed to arise from having been drafted or from fighting a war? Why is launching a business to become rich considered superficial? Does an enterprise that generates large earnings thereby lose worth?

Wolf's warning against a focus on achieving "ease, prestige, and material wealth" is ironic, given that, as any academic dean knows, the tried-and-true method of recruiting professors is to offer them the ease most of them find in a reduced teaching schedule, the prestige of joining other well-known colleagues, and a sizable increase in salary. Trying to persuade noted scholars to join a department without offering them greater ease, prestige, or material wealth is not likely to succeed.

As for hobbies, collecting rubber bands is no doubt unusual, but people have devoted their lives to collecting stamps, coins, baseball memorabilia, beer bottles, theatrical programs, medieval works in astrology, and comic books. Are some collections meaningful and others not?

One philosopher we know has devoted innumerable hours to practicing and playing golf. Another friend, also a philosopher, finds golf an utter waste of time. Is one of them right and the other wrong?

Wolf suggests that "mindless, futile, never-ending tasks" are not likely to be meaningful.[7] These criteria, however, are questionable. For instance, running on a treadmill is mindless, trying to persuade all others of your solutions to philosophical problems is futile, and seeking to eliminate all disease is never-ending. Are these activities, therefore, without meaning? Lifting heavier and heavier weights may be mindless, futile, and never-ending, but we see no reason to derogate weightlifting.

Why not allow others to pursue their own ways of life without disparaging their choices and declaring their lives meaningless? After all, others might declare meaningless a life devoted to philosophical speculation that leads to writing articles that leads to others reading those articles that leads to more philosophical speculation that leads to writing more articles that leads to others reading more articles. Why is such activity more meaningful than that engaged in by Wiggins's pig farmers?

The tangle in which Wolf finds herself is apparent in her explanation of why Woody Allen, in his movie *Manhattan,* includes in the protagonist's list of things that make life worth living the crabs at Sam Woo's. She hypothesizes that Allen "regards the dish as an accomplishment meriting aesthetic appreciation."[8] A simpler, more obvious explanation is that he finds the crabs tasty.

Wolf herself admits that she enjoys eating chocolate, exercising in aerobics class, and playing computer games.[9] Why, then, does she insist on devaluing these activities? After all, if a person can find delights that bring no harm, such a discovery should be appreciated, not denigrated.

A fundamental question about Wolf's approach is whether in her view individuals are the best judges of the worth of their own lives. Here Wolf waffles. She speaks of a need "to see one's life as valuable in a way that can be recognized from a point of view other than one's own." Yet "no one need accept someone else's word for what has objective value."[10]

In what way, then, are we to decide which activities are of worth? Wolf's suggestion is that "we are likely to make the most progress toward an answer if we pool our information and experience."[11] How to proceed with such a collaborative inquiry is unclear.

Even with all these problems, however, Wolf's theory faces an even more daunting difficulty, which appears when she tries to address a criticism of her theory from psychologist Jonathan Haidt. As a counterexample to her claim that a meaningful life requires focus on "objects worthy of love,"[12] he presents the case of one of his students, a shy woman who was passionate about horses: riding them, studying their history, and making " 'horse friends' " with others who shared her passion. Haidt argues that this woman found meaning in life through her interest in horses, but he recognizes that "all of her horsing around does nothing for anyone else, and it does not make the world a better place."[13] Thus, according to Haidt, in this case Wolf's theory of objective value fails.

Remembering the long list of activities whose worth Wolf does not accept, we might anticipate that she would dismiss horses as an inappropriate subject on which to build a significant life. Surprisingly, however, she agrees with Haidt that horses might contribute to the meaningfulness of the woman's life. The reason Wolf offers is that a person's liking some activity, whatever it may be, can lead to its becoming valuable for that individual.

But then what becomes of objective value? Wolf senses the problem and admits that her discussion "may leave others either disappointed by what they see as a watering down of what is distinctive about my conception of meaningfulness or confused about what the point of it is, if it is to be understood so broadly."[14]

Such confusion is understandable, especially when Wolf goes on to find the possibility of objective value in lawn mower-racing, being a basketball fan, and even solving crossword puzzles, the same activity she had previously declared meaningless. No wonder Wolf warns us that her views "will be of little or no *practical* use."[15]

This limitation is clear if we try to apply Wolf's views to the cases of Pat and Lee. After all, if riding horses, racing lawn mowers, being a sports fan, and solving crossword puzzles might give meaning to life, then Pat can surely find meaning in teaching, playing bridge, and practicing the cello, while Lee can find meaning in swimming, driving luxury cars, and traveling to distant locations.

Is one of these individuals living a more worthwhile life than the other? Trying to resolve this question by determining who has undertaken projects of worth does not provide the answer we seek.

4

FLOURISHING?

Another strategy is adopted by Richard Kraut, who identifies living well with "flourishing." He uses that term to characterize a human being "who possesses, develops, and enjoys the exercise of cognitive, affective, sensory, and social powers (no less than physical powers)." Those who flourish develop "properly and fully" the "potentialities, capacities, and faculties that (under favorable conditions) they naturally have at an early stage of their existence."[1]

This approach, however, raises a series of problems. First, not all our potentials can be actualized in a single lifetime. An individual who might have the talents to succeed as an organist, football player, surgeon, stockbroker, or engineer does not have the time to fulfill all these goals at a high level. Choices need be made, and in every case some possibilities will remain unfulfilled.

Furthermore, how do we know at an early stage of a person's existence which abilities that individual may develop later in life? Consider Anna Mary Moses (1860–1961), who was a farmer's wife in Virginia and New York and did embroidery of country scenes. At the age of seventy-five she began to paint, achieving worldwide fame as "Grandma Moses." She was not born to be a painter or a farmer's wife. She had a range of abilities and opportunities, and over time made her choices.

No appeal to what is natural will demonstrate what ought to be. As Sidney Hook writes, "What man should be is undoubtedly related to what he is, for no man should be what he cannot be. Yet a proposition about what he is no more uniquely entails what he should be than the recognition of the nature of an egg necessitates our concluding that the egg should become a chicken rather than an egg sandwich."[2]

Furthermore, not all our abilities are worthy. As Kraut himself puts it, "some natural powers are bad for the person who has them." Skills as a liar, cheater, and hypocrite are presumably among those Kraut believes should be "extirpated."[3]

Which abilities, then, should we develop? Kraut answers that we should develop those that lead to flourishing. But which ones lead to flourishing? Those that are good. And which are good? Those that lead to flourishing. This circularity doesn't help us choose from among the options we face.

To illustrate the problem, consider the real-life case of Phil Saltman, a jazz pianist in the 1930s and 1940s, whose extraordinary talents could have propelled him to international renown.[4] After appearing as soloist with the Boston Pops Orchestra, however, he decided that life as a touring musician was not to his liking. He chose instead to open a summer camp for boys and girls who enjoyed playing music, even if they did not plan to pursue the activity professionally. The camp succeeded,[5] and he never doubted his choice to give up the opportunity for a distinguished solo career in order to guide youngsters and play music with them in amateur combos.

Did he make a mistake? Did he limit his chances for a successful life? Did he waste his significant talents?

Kraut would have answered that he should have chosen to flourish. But would he have flourished more by pursuing a concert career or by becoming a camp director? Some of his friends thought he had made a serious mistake; others agreed with his choice. No appeal to the concept of flourishing, however, would have helped settle the matter.

Perhaps more insight can be found in the specific examples Kraut offers. Let us, therefore, consider the activities he cites with strong approval, as well as those about which he shows much less enthusiasm.

Among those he favors are walking, dancing, traveling, playing tennis, swimming, attending the opera, writing poetry, reading novels, basking in the warmth of the sun, cooking, doing crossword puzzles, playing chess, running an organization, philosophizing, and enjoying our sexual powers.[6] Ones he finds of lesser value include bowling, playing checkers, watching inane television programs, accumulating wealth, achieving fame, holding socially isolating jobs, and remaining single.[7]

As with Susan Wolf's account of meaningful and meaningless activities, Kraut's lists raise more questions than they answer. Why is tennis better than bowling? How do both compare to badminton, archery, or quoits? Why is chess better than checkers? Perhaps Kraut would find checkers more challenging if he had lost game after game to a checkers champion. Which game's value is more akin to that of Scrabble? What's the matter with socially isolating jobs? Serving as a lighthouse keeper, exploring a rainforest, writing fiction in a remote cabin, or doing research in a library cubicle are surely worthy activities.

Why does Kraut, as did Wolf, denigrate fame and wealth? We doubt either of them would reject a professorial position on the grounds that the institution offering it provides too much status or an excessively high salary.

Why does the study of philosophy invariably appear on philosophers' lists of worthwhile activities? Indeed, the study of such subjects as sociology, geology, Asian religions, ceramics, and finance are rarely cited with enthusiasm.

Kraut contrasts checkers and literature, finding little value in the former but much in the latter. If a person delights in playing board games, however, and does not particularly enjoy reading the novels of Henry James or Thomas Hardy, should we conclude, as Kraut does, that the individual "is handicapped by a cognitive or linguistic disability"?[8] Should we also say that anyone not fond of lieder is handicapped by a musical disability?

Why is Kraut against the single life? He suggests that a person might wish to marry because of thinking that "the complex affective and interactive skills needed by a good marriage partner are ones that he will enjoy acquiring and exercising." (Perhaps such words would not be the most inspiring to recite at a wedding.) Could the single life also have advantages? Kraut doesn't suggest any. However, he strongly supports sexual activity, maintaining that "The extinction of sexual desire, in favorable circumstances—that is, when there are attractive and likable people to whom one can give and from whom one can receive sexual pleasure—would be a great loss."[9] The dubious implication is that chastity, whether for moral, religious, or personal reasons, is not conducive to flourishing.

Do all Kraut's examples help decide whether Pat or Lee is living a more worthwhile life? Kraut, not surprisingly, expresses much enthusiasm for what he terms "the thrilling *process* of acquiring a body of knowledge about a subject that fascinates us."[10] Thus we can assume he would judge that Pat the philosopher is flourishing, especially because Pat is married, plays the cello, and enjoys strolling the beaches of Cape Cod.

Perhaps surprisingly, however, many of Kraut's criteria for flourishing also fit Lee's life. Lee enjoys swimming and the warmth of the sun. Lee's physical powers have been developed by surfing and golfing, while Lee's cognitive and sensory powers have been increased by travel. Moreover, Lee's social powers have been enhanced through many friendships, and Lee's affective powers are developed from numerous romances. As to "enjoyment of sexual powers," Lee's accomplishments in this area likely have exceeded those of Pat.

How, then, are we to weigh Lee's advantages against Pat's devotion to teaching, research, family, and hobbies? Assuming Lee sometimes reads literature and does not spend much time playing checkers, Lee, like Pat, would meet Kraut's criteria for flourishing. Thus we have made no progress in deciding which of the two, if either, is closer to living well.

5

THINGS THAT MATTER?

Assuming that lists of more and less worthwhile activities offer too easy a target for criticism, why not avoid specifics and simply assert that living well is pursuing goals of intrinsic value? Such a strategy is adopted by Stephen Darwall, who claims that "the best life for human beings is one of significant engagement in activities through which we come into appreciative rapport with agent-neutral values, such as aesthetic beauty, knowledge and understanding, and the worth of living beings." These values are "intrinsically worthy of esteem and admiration."[1]

Darwall here fails to take into account John Dewey's insight that any activity can have intrinsic value. In Dewey's words, "We can imagine a man who at one time thoroughly enjoys converse with his friends; at another the hearing of a symphony; at another the eating of his meals; at another the reading of a book; at another the earning of money, and so on. As an appreciative realization, each of these is an intrinsic value. It occupies a particular place in life; it serves its own end, which cannot be supplied by a substitute."[2] In other words, depending on the specific situation, any good may be viewed as of intrinsic worth and not a means to something else. Thus sometimes Pat may consider philosophy, bridge, or playing the cello to have intrinsic value, while Lee may think the same of surfing, golf, or travel.

Darwall, however, adds that our activities are meritorious only if others recognize them as such. Therefore we should focus on "things that matter," and things matter only if others who care about us judge that our choices "have worth."[3] Do Pat's friends find Pat's life to be of worth? Quite likely. Do Lee's friends find Lee's life to be of worth? Also quite likely. Thus we again reach an impasse.

Even if those who care about us are unanimous about the course we should follow, relying on such a test of our decisions is inappropriate. To see why, consider another real-life case, that of a woman named Judy, who thought of becoming a philosopher. She tried graduate studies but received little encouragement from her teachers. Hence she quit school and joined an advertising firm as a copywriting trainee. Not particularly successful there, she worked next as a ghostwriter on a book about the American public-school system.

Imagine at this point she had asked those who cared about her how she should proceed with her life. Should she return to advertising, continue as a ghostwriter, try philosophy again, or instead get married and start a family? Suppose all those who cared about her had considered the matter conscientiously and advised her to choose the last option. Perhaps they doubted her chances for professional success in the fields she had explored, and therefore urged her to focus on the challenges of parenting, agreeing with Darwall that it "is a noble pursuit, it has merit, because it appropriately responds to the importance of children, their significance or worth."[4] We don't know what advice her friends offered, but, regardless, she made up her own mind and decided to try again to succeed in academic life. She surely did, becoming one of the world's foremost philosophers: Judith Jarvis Thomson.[5]

Her decision was wise, although had she chosen differently the outcome might also have been positive. Furthermore, other individuals with their own abilities and interests might better have proceeded otherwise. None of these judgments, however, would have been aided by Darwall's advice to seek "active engagement with and appreciation of values whose worth transcends their capacity to benefit (extrinsically or intrinsically)."[6] Would that principle have ruled out Judith Jarvis Thomson's becoming a leading advertising executive? We have no idea.

In developing his position, Darwall cites a photograph of the late pianist David Golub, who, we are told, is accompanying two vocalists. Golub is smiling, and Darwall comments, "I imagine that what his smile primarily reveals is an appreciation of values that *make* music-making a noble pursuit—values like the aesthetic qualities of the music he and his colleagues are making, values that give music importance, significance, or *worth*. And I imagine that the benefit he derives from playing comes, in large measure, through a vivid sense of this worth and his relation to it."[7]

First, remember that if Golub, while playing a recital, is thinking about anything other than the details of the music, he would not be a successful accompanist. The task is too difficult to allow attention to wander, and reflecting on non-musical matters is courting disaster. Second, many performers in a variety of fields smile: politicians, entertainers, skaters, clowns. What do their smiles tell us about the value of their activities? Nothing. Third, in many undertakings, participants who fulfill their responsibilities rarely smile: performing surgery, catching a criminal, serving on a jury, making a tough business decision, meeting a journalistic deadline, driving a race car, or repairing a broken pipe. What does a lack of smiling while working reveal about these endeavors? Again, nothing. In short, interpreting a smile offers no help in defending a theory of value.

Darwall, of course, would have found merit in Thomson's career choice, because, like Wolf and Kraut, he takes philosophy as a paradigm case of a worthwhile undertaking. As he puts it, "Readers of this essay might agree that philosophy and philosophical activity have intrinsic worth."[8]

No doubt most would concur. Keep in mind, however, the insightful words of the pre-Socratic philosopher Xenophanes, who is said to have remarked that "if oxen and horses and lions had hands, and could draw with their hands and do what man can do, horses would draw the gods in the shape of horses, and oxen in the shape of oxen, each giving the gods bodies similar to their own."[9]

Of course, most philosophers find philosophy to be worthwhile, just as most chess players find chess to be worthwhile. After all, how many of us suppose that living well depends on engaging in activities that we do not enjoy or may hardly understand? Instead, we are prone to urge others to recognize the worth of at least some of our preferred endeavors. For instance, philosophers rarely fight fires, achieve extraordinary feats of athleticism, or amass large sums of money in business ventures. Few philosophers, therefore, are apt to find as much value in firefighting, professional sports, or commerce as in contemplation.

The high regard in which philosophers hold philosophy, an attitude historically associated with Aristotle,[10] has been expressed in strong terms by Neil Levy. He argues that among the best of all lives is the pursuit of knowledge, exemplified in philosophical inquiry, which to his mind is an activity open only to an elite, fortunate enough to possess "cognitive abilities of a special sort, which are . . . extremely sophisticated *relative* to the population norm."[11]

The supposition that academics, especially philosophers, are more intelligent than all others is not likely to survive witnessing even one faculty meeting. Nevertheless, Levy is committed to the view that work as a physician, judge, business executive, airline pilot, artist, electrician, caregiver, or parent ranks below spending countless hours assessing issues in metaphysics or epistemology. We find this implication to be a *reductio ad absurdum* of his position.

Now let us return to assessing the lives of Pat and Lee. We reject the assumption—common to Wolf, Kraut, and Darwall—that for all people at all times, certain activities are intrinsically more worthy than others. Matters are not clarified by appeal to "projects of worth," "flourishing," or "things that matter." To assess lives, we need to find a more promising approach.

6

MORALITY AND HAPPINESS

Despite the vast differences in the interests of Pat and Lee, both act morally, and neither harms anyone. Furthermore, Pat shows concern for colleagues and students, while Lee is kind to friends and donates generously to worthy causes. Indeed, were Pat and Lee unethical, they would not be living well.

To speak, as Harry Frankfurt does, of Nazism offering its leaders a "complex, exhilarating, and rewarding life"[1] is unconvincing. Value cannot be found in doing unmitigated evil. Nor, as Richard Taylor apparently overlooks, can the desire to act immorally provide the basis for a good life. Fame and fortune may come to those who are immoral, but their lives do not deserve to be judged positively by anyone with moral compunctions.

How is acting morally connected to achieving happiness? Some philosophers, echoing Plato, have argued that those who are moral are happy, and those who are happy are moral.

Among the many who believe happiness depends on a commitment to morality is Philippa Foot. While she finds happiness "a most intractable concept," she defends the claim that "great happiness, unlike euphoria or even great pleasure, must come from something related to what is deep in human nature, and fundamental in human life, such as affection for children and friends, the desire to work, and love of freedom and truth."[2] Thus she believes immorality precludes happiness. We, however, are not persuaded by her claim and offer the following counterexample.

Consider Fred, a fictitious person but an amalgamation of several individuals we have known. Fred's life has been devoted to achieving three aims: fame, wealth, and a reputation for probity. He has no interest whatsoever in friends or truth. Indeed, he is treacherous and thoroughly dishonest. Nevertheless, he has attained his three goals and is, in fact, a rich celebrity renowned for his supposed integrity. His acquiring a good name while acting unscrupulously is a tribute to his audacity, cunning, and luck. Now he rests self-satisfied: basking in renown, delighting in luxuries, and relishing praise for his reputed commitment to the highest moral standards.

That he enjoys great pleasure, even euphoria, is undeniable. According to Foot, however, he is not happy. We rather would say that *we* are not happy with *him*. We do not wish to see shallowness and hypocrisy rewarded. Indeed, while numerous works of literature describe good persons who are doomed to failure, few works tell of evil persons who ultimately triumph. (An exception to the rule is Natasha in Chekov's *The Three Sisters*, a play that causes anguish to most audiences.)

We can define "happiness" so as to falsify the claim that Fred is happy. This philosophical "sleight-of-hand," though, accomplishes little, for Fred is wholly contented, suffering no worries or anxieties. Indeed, he is smug as he revels in his exalted position.

Surely Fred is happy. Perhaps later in life he won't be. Or perhaps he will. He may come to the end of his days as happy as he is now. That prospect affords us no comfort but may nevertheless come to pass. (Incidentally, the name "Fred," to which we shall refer occasionally, can be remembered as an acronym derived from the words "fame," "riches," "esteem," and "deceit.")

Not all philosophers agree with us that Fred is happy. They admit he is "feeling happy"[3] or is "happy in some limited way,"[4] but they deny he is "truly happy"[5] or has attained "real happiness."[6]

To be sure, language can be revised to suit our purposes. In the memorable words of Humpty Dumpty, "When *I* use a word, it means just what I choose it to mean—neither more nor less."[7] Thus if any philosopher wishes to use the word "happiness" in a special way, reserving it for situations in which a person who is deeply satisfied with life is also virtuous, then that philosopher is free to engage in linguistic revision. Doing, so, however, can easily mislead, for when an ordinary word is given a nonstandard use, those who hear it are apt to suppose that the word means what it usually means, thus leading to confusion.

Suppose, for instance, you are told that a student is happy to be enrolled in a particular college. Ordinarily we would infer from that statement that the student likes attending the college but not that the student has earned high grades. We could decide, of course, that students are to be considered happy at college only if they receive high grades, but such non-standard usage would lead to perplexity, as people would wonder why a student without high grades could not be happy at college.

One historical reason why some philosophers may suppose happiness requires moral behavior is that Aristotle in his *Nicomachean Ethics* claims that *eudaimonia*, a Greek word often translated as "happiness," can be achieved only by virtuous activity, the fulfillment of the best aspect of human nature. Hence an immoral person cannot be happy, because that person has not attained the finest end for humanity. (Later in the *Nicomachean Ethics* Aristotle maintains that the best life for a human being is a life of contemplation, thus giving rise to the scholarly issue of how to reconcile Aristotle's two accounts of happiness. We accept the truth of neither, so for us the issue is moot.)

To translate *eudaimonia* as "happiness," however, is misleading, precisely because the English word "happiness" does not imply good intentions or virtuous action. Perhaps *eudaimonia* would better be understood as pertaining to "admirable activity," because the English word "admirable" has implications of worthiness. Happiness, however, is only worthy if its source is worthy. An unethical person may find happiness in immoral actions; indeed, deriving satisfaction from deeds that lack compassion is the essence of immorality. Some people, unfortunately, lack regard for anyone else, but to claim they are not only immoral but unhappy is misleading, suggesting that they find no satisfaction in their behavior, even if they do.

Instead, we shall use the term "happiness" in its ordinary sense, referring to a state of contentment in which an individual is not disquieted or disturbed but has found deep satisfaction. In this sense a person can be more or less happy, happier at one time than another, happy regardless of level of intelligence, happy and moral, or happy and immoral.

Why have so many philosophers, past and present, been loath to admit the last possibility, that of a happy immoralist? We believe they rightly regard the concept as a threat to morality. For the greater the divergence between morality and happiness, the greater the loss of motivation to choose the moral path. Trying to define the happy immoralist out of existence is one way to reach a preferred conclusion.

Despite such linguistic reform, however, the wicked may prosper and find contentment while doing so. Moreover, the good may suffer and find unhappiness. Few philosophers follow Plato in trying to argue against the latter claim. Indeed, the travails of the righteous are, as we indicated, a common theme in literature.

Perhaps the most famous example is found in the Book of Job. Here Job, a man of exemplary piety and extraordinary good fortune, is the subject of a wager between God and Satan. The latter scoffs at Job's devoutness, claiming that Job is obedient to God only because God has given Job good health, a fine family, and untold wealth. Although God testifies to Job's goodness, God permits Satan to test Job by causing him to suffer the severest personal losses. Suddenly all ten of Job's children die, and his wealth is destroyed. When Job does not relinquish his faith in God, Satan, claiming that Job has maintained his faith only because his own body has been spared, obtains further permission from God to inflict on Job a painful disease.

Job's friends believe Job is suffering as a result of having sinned, because they believe that God does not punish the innocent. Yet readers know that in this case such is exactly what has happened. When God eventually appears to answer Job's cries for an explanation of these events, God doesn't reveal the truth—that Job was the subject of a bet with Satan—but emphasizes, instead, the utter insignificance of humanity and its inability to understand the workings of the Almighty. Job is overawed. Then God rebukes Job's friends for the erroneous advice they offered, and heals Job, restoring to him twice as much wealth as he had possessed before his misfortunes, and blessing him with ten children and a long and happy life. Of course, the ten children who are given to Job at the end of the story may to some extent compensate Job for his previous losses, but the dead children are not compensated. They are not restored to life.

In sum, the Book of Job stands opposed to the prevailing theology of much of the rest of the Hebrew Bible. The doctrine of retributive justice, presented in Deuteronomy, Psalms, Proverbs, and elsewhere, states that a pious person will be rewarded with wealth and happiness; a sinner will suffer both economic and physical adversity. The Book of Job is a criticism of this supposition.

Even readers who may offer a different interpretation of the story of Job do not deny that bad things may happen to good people. Similarly, good things may happen to bad people. Such is the case of Fred.

7

MORALITY AND UNHAPPINESS

S ome commentators have found fault with our account of Fred because they suppose that Fred's happiness is "fragile,"[1] his situation "perilous,"[2] and his reputation "vulnerable to exposure."[3] No doubt circumstances can be imagined in which things go badly for Fred, but we can also imagine circumstances in which immoral behavior provides a greater chance to avoid disaster than does acting morally. Here is an example inspired by the plot of Woody Allen's thought-provoking movie *Crimes and Misdemeanors*.

Suppose a man who is happily married and highly respected as a physician makes the mistake of embarking on an affair with an unmarried woman whom he meets while she is working as a flight attendant. When he tries to break off this relationship, she threatens to expose his adultery and thereby wreck his marriage and career.

All he has worked for his entire life is at risk. He knows that if the affair is revealed, his wife will divorce him, his children will reject him, and the members of his community will no longer support his medical practice. Instead of being the object of people's admiration, he will be viewed with scorn. In short, his life will be shattered.

As the flight attendant is about to take the steps that will destroy him, he confides in his brother, who has connections to the criminal underworld. The brother offers to help him by arranging for the flight attendant to be murdered, with minimal danger that the crime will be traced to either the physician or his brother.

Should the physician consent to the killing? Doing so is clearly immoral, but, if all goes as planned, he will avoid calamity.

The physician agrees to the murder, and when it is carried out and the police investigate, they attribute it to a drifter who eventually dies of alcoholism, and the case is closed. The physician's life goes on without further complications from the matter, and years later he is honored at a testimonial dinner where, accompanied by his loving wife and adoring children, he accepts the effusive gratitude of the community for his lifetime of service. He is a happy man, taking pride in both the affection of his family and the admiration of his patients and friends.

Even most of those who might take issue with our claim that the physician is happy would agree that he is happier than he would have been had his life been destroyed. Hence his immorality enhanced his chances for happiness.

Yet what if his role in the murder had been discovered? Wasn't he taking a chance? Of course, but if we leave aside considerations of morality and focus on issues of strategy, the likelihood of catastrophe would have been greater if he had allowed his adultery to become known. Murder is more dangerous than adultery, but in this case the odds were that the adultery would be made public, while the murder would not.

Wouldn't his conscience bother him? In *Crimes and Misdemeanors* that question is asked and answered in a conversation between the physician, Judah Rosenthal (played by Martin Landau), and the questioner, a documentary filmmaker named Cliff Stern (played by Woody Allen). As the story nears its conclusion, they discuss the scenario hypothetically.

In responding to Cliff's suggestion that the murderer would be hard-pressed to live with his choice, Judah admits the murderer would be plagued by guilt, but "then one morning he awakens. The sun is shining, and his family is around him. Mysteriously the crisis is lifted. He takes his family on vacation to Europe, and as the months pass, he finds he's not punished. In fact, he prospers. . . . Now he's scot-free. His life is completely back to normal." When Cliff doubts that the murderer could go back in this way, Judah replies, "Well, people carry sins around with them. . . . Oh, maybe once in a while he has a bad moment, but it passes. And with time, it all fades." Cliff insists that the murderer should turn himself in so that the story would assume tragic proportions. Judah responds, "But that's fiction. That's movies. You see too many movies. I'm talking about reality. I mean, if you want a happy ending, you should go see a Hollywood movie."

While everyone's happiness is fragile, given the ever-present possibilities of accident, illness, and death, isn't the happiness of those who act immorally more fragile than the happiness of those who act morally? On average such is the case, but averages don't necessarily apply in specific cases. For instance, the average man is taller than the average woman, but some women are taller than most men. Judah Rosenthal's adultery made his happiness especially perilous, but once he was threatened with exposure of his affair, even greater immorality was arguably his best chance to avoid utter disaster. Thus specific circumstances determine whether the risk inherent in an immoral action is offset by the probability of escape from an otherwise hopeless situation.

A well-known piece of political wisdom is that the cover-up of a crime is more likely to bring trouble than the crime itself. Rarely mentioned, however, is that the cover-up may succeed, thereby keeping the crime under wraps.

The situation is akin to that of a poker player holding a weak hand who decides to bluff. Doing so may cause the player to lose more money than need be, but at the same time the bluff may work, thereby turning a poor hand into a winning one. The better the poker player, the better a sense of when to bluff.

8

CHARACTER

Some philosophers have argued that Fred could not be happy because friendships are necessary for happiness, and Fred has no interest in friends. Christopher W. Gowans, for instance, imagines Fred "sitting alone watching himself praised on his wide-screen television." Does he not feel "lonely"?[1]

To begin with, the assumption that having friends is essential for happiness is implausible. Some people prefer solitude. They would rather eat alone than with others. They like to travel by themselves, not in a group. They work solo rather than collaboratively. Granted, friends can provide support, but they also can be a source of unwanted obligations. Hence while most of us seek friends and are unhappy without them, a few people reject any overture to intense involvements. They prefer privacy to intimacy.

Fred, however, isn't a lone wolf. He's friendly with innumerable people, doing favors for many and receiving favors in return. He is expert at socializing, for how else could he win support, make successful deals, and earn widespread praise for his supposed integrity?

Does he care about others? No. Do others realize his lack of concern? No. Remember, he's a phony but a successful one.

Do we correctly assess the character of all those with whom we interact? Surely not. Here is one reason, for example, why national searches for academic administrators often produce disappointing results. A candidate who appears confident and genial may turn out in office to be evasive or irresponsible. Another whose crusty manner or candid opinions make a poor first impression may nevertheless be given the opportunity to serve in an administrative position and become widely admired for trustworthiness and conscientiousness. The lesson is that cordiality doesn't guarantee honesty.

Fred's true character is unknown to the public as well as to some, although not all, who work with him. If asked, many would say Fred had numerous friends, including themselves. After all, such is his act, and he performs it with panache.

We may think we know people well, yet be surprised by their decisions. To illustrate with a realistic case, suppose as a professor you write letters of recommendation for two of your outstanding graduate students, Joan and Kate, who are seeking faculty positions. You praise both for the high quality of their scholarship, their skill in teaching, their fine characters, and their amiable personalities. Later you learn that Kate obtained an attractive academic position but Joan found none and reluctantly left academia. You wonder about this outcome, but lacking an explanation, attribute it to luck.

The situation, however, involves choice, not merely chance. Joan, in fact, was interviewed at a first-rate school and during her visit was told by the dean that the job was hers. The dean, however, had one condition: Joan was expected to teach a particular course each year in which numerous varsity athletes would enroll, and she would be required to award them all passing grades, even if their work was in every respect unsatisfactory. Only the dean would know of this special arrangement.

Joan rejected the position on moral grounds and continued trying to obtain a suitable opportunity in academic life. Never again, however, was she offered a faculty position, and she was forced to pursue a career path that gave her little satisfaction. Her potential as a teacher went unfulfilled, and her planned research was left undone. Throughout her life she remained embittered.

Kate was invited for an interview at the school Joan had turned down, and the dean made her the identical offer made to Joan. After weighing the options, Kate accepted the appointment, even though she recognized that doing so would require her to act unethically.

Kate went on to a highly successful academic career, became a popular teacher and renowned researcher, moved to one of the nation's most prestigious universities, and enjoyed all the perquisites attendant to her membership on that school's renowned faculty. Occasionally she recalled the conditions of her initial appointment but viewed the actions she had taken as an unfortunate but necessary step on her path to a wonderful life.

How Joan and Kate would each handle the dean's offer was hard to predict, for a person's character is not always manifest. Clearly, however, the case illustrates again that happiness and morality do not necessarily go together. As Bernard Gert concludes, "a person does not need to be moral in order to be happy or to live a fulfilling life."[2]

APPEARING MORAL

Although happiness and morality are conceptually independent, an empirical connection exists between a person's moral character and happiness. Because most of us desire to develop and sustain relationships with others who will be more likely to react positively to us if we are kind and trustworthy, being moral enhances our potential for happiness. Alternatively, a person's nastiness and treachery will win few friends. (Fred, after all, was not only crafty but lucky.)

We are not denying the possibility of a happy tyrant, a happy hermit, or a happy immoralist; to be happy, however, most of us rely on the good will of others. Psychologists studying happiness have found a positive correlation between people's social contacts (including family and friends) and the level of satisfaction with life. As psychologist Michael Argyle notes, "In many studies [social relationships] come out as the greatest single source of happiness."[1] Thus, although acting immorally might result in short-term gains, in the long run it is likely to besmirch our reputations and undermine our contentment.

A crucial issue often overlooked, however, is whether we benefit from actually being moral or merely appearing to be moral (like Fred). The virtuous person is bound by moral obligations and hence unable to capitalize on opportunities to increase happiness through immoral actions. The individual who merely appears to be virtuous might enjoy exactly the same advantages in reputation gained by someone who is genuinely virtuous but will be able to exploit situations in which immorality enhances happiness. Thus maximizing happiness could result not from being moral but appearing to be moral.

To develop this point more fully, consider these four cases: (1) a moral person who appears to be moral; (2) an immoral person who appears to be moral; (3) a moral person who appears to be immoral; and (4) an immoral person who appears to be immoral.

Case 4 is worst for the individual. The blatant immoralist may be able to achieve some limited goals but once recognized as immoral will likely face unhappiness, as a result of social disapproval or even time in jail.

Case 3, a moral person who appears to be immoral, is almost as bad for promoting happiness. Although such individuals can take pride in knowing they are acting morally, they will nevertheless suffer the negative consequences associated with the blatant immoralist.

Suppose that Linda, an attorney who believes that justice requires all those charged with a crime to have competent counsel, agrees to defend a terrorist accused of a murderous bombing. Linda has no sympathy for the deadly attack but does her best in the interests of her client. The public, however, fails to appreciate her position and views her as a terrorist sympathizer. Threats are made against Linda and her family, and she is eventually forced to give up her practice and move to another locale. She has acted morally and may receive personal satisfaction from having taken a courageous stand, but because the public views her actions as immoral, she has impaired her happiness, just as she would have had she acted immorally.

Case 1, a moral person who appears to be moral, offers a commonly accepted model for achieving happiness but still has drawbacks. In those circumstances in which happiness depends on acting immorally, the moral person will be forced to sacrifice happiness for the sake of morality. Do such circumstances actually arise? As we have seen, only those in the grip of an unrealistic philosophical theory deny the possibility.

Consider Ann, who is invited to a concert that takes place simultaneously with her sister's moving to a new apartment. Ann had promised to help her sister move, but the performers are Ann's favorite, and this appearance is their last engagement before they disband. Ann does not want to miss this once-in-a-lifetime opportunity, but her sister would be greatly upset if Ann breaks her promise. What should she do?

As a virtuous person she has no choice but to honor her commitment, thus sacrificing her happiness. If, however, she were not virtuous, she might fabricate a compelling excuse and be happier. Some might suppose that Ann's lie would in some way bring her unhappiness, but that assumption, while perhaps comforting, is unwarranted. We could tell a story about how Ann's breaking her promise worked out badly for her and her sister, but we could tell an equally plausible tale about how lying worked out well for both of them.

Sometimes the path of morality leads to misery. For instance, someone may stop to help a stranger fix a flat tire, only to be hit by an oncoming truck. Similarly, a whistle-blower who tells the truth may be fired, while a politician who refuses to vote against conscience may thereby forfeit a realistic chance for reelection. In such cases the individual's happiness is lost as a result of adhering to ethical standards.

In case 2, however, an immoral person who appears to be moral, the subject possesses all the advantages of a reputation for honesty while avoiding the disadvantages of always acting as morality dictates. Such an individual retains the option of acting immorally whenever greater personal happiness would result. Admittedly, the person takes a risk because exposure might bring ruin, but by striving to develop the reputation of being moral, and acting immorally only when the payoff is huge and the chances of being caught are small, the crafty immoralist may find more happiness than anyone else.

Faced with this conclusion, some philosophers focus on cases of extreme depravity, then make the obvious point that such behavior is less preferable than adherence to morality. The more realistic option that confronts each person, though, is not whether to choose unmitigated evils but whether to do wrong when such action offers a likely means to happiness. When we face a critical decision in what may be highly tempting circumstances, we are, as Jean-Paul Sartre writes, "condemned to be free."[2]

At this point many are apt to look to God to find a reason why we should act morally, even if doing so is likely to lead to personal unhappiness. God, it is said, has made clear the moral path, and we should act in accord with God's will. This line of argument has wide appeal and deserves careful consideration.

GOD AND MORALITY

According to many religions (although not all), the world was created by God, an all-powerful, all-knowing, all-good being. Although God's existence has been doubted, let us for the moment assume its truth. What implications of this supposition would be relevant to our lives?

Some people would feel more secure in the knowledge that the world had been planned by an all-good being. Others would feel insecure, realizing the extent to which their existence depended on a decision of this being. In any case, most people, out of either fear or respect, would wish to act in accord with God's will.

Belief in God by itself, however, provides no hint whatsoever of which actions God wishes us to perform or what we ought to do to please or obey God. We may affirm that God is all-good, yet have no way of knowing the highest moral standards. All we may presume is that, whatever these standards, God always acts in accordance with them. We might expect God to have implanted the correct moral standards in our minds, but this supposition is doubtful in view of the conflicts among people's intuitions. Furthermore, even if consensus prevailed, it might be only a means by which God tests us to see whether we have the courage to dissent from popular opinion.

Some would argue that if God exists, then murder is immoral, because it destroys what God with infinite wisdom created. This argument, however, fails on several grounds. First, God also created germs, viruses, and disease-carrying rats. Because God created these things, ought they not be eliminated? Second, if God arranged for us to live, God also arranged for us to die. By killing, are we assisting the work of God? Third, God provided us with the mental and physical potential to commit murder. Does God wish us to fulfill this potential?

Thus God's existence alone does not imply any particular moral precepts. We may hope our actions are in accord with God's standards, but no test is available to check whether what we do is best in God's eyes. As we have noted, some good people suffer great ills, whereas some seemingly evil people achieve happiness. Perhaps in a future life these outcomes will be reversed, but we have no way of ascertaining who, if anyone, is ultimately punished and who ultimately rewarded.

Over the course of history, those who believed in God's existence typically were eager to learn God's will and tended to rely on those individuals who claimed to possess such insight. Diviners, seers, and priests were given positions of great influence. Competition among them was severe, however, for no one could be sure which oracle to believe.

In any case, prophets died, and their supposedly revelatory powers disappeared with them. For practical purposes, what was needed was a permanent record of God's will. This requirement was met by the writing of holy books in which God's will was revealed to all.

But even though many such books were supposed to embody the will of God, they conflicted with one another. Which was to be accepted? Belief in the existence of God by itself yields no answer.

Let us suppose, however, that an individual becomes persuaded that a reliable guide to God's will is contained in the Ten

Commandments. This person, therefore, believes that to murder, steal, or commit adultery is wrong.

But why is it wrong? Is it wrong because God says so, or does God say so because it is wrong?

This crucial issue was raised more than two thousand years ago in Plato's remarkable dialogue, the *Euthyphro*. Plato's teacher, Socrates, who in most of Plato's works is given the leading role, asks the overconfident Euthyphro whether actions are right because God says they are right, or whether God says actions are right because they are right.

In other words, Socrates is inquiring whether actions are right because of God's fiat or whether God is subject to moral standards. If actions are right because of God's command, then anything God commands would be right. Had God commanded adultery, stealing, and murder, then adultery, stealing, and murder would be right—surely an unsettling and to many an unacceptable conclusion.

Granted, some may be willing to adopt this discomforting view, but then they face another difficulty. If the good is whatever God commands, to say that God's commands are good amounts to saying that God's commands are God's commands, a mere tautology or repetition of words. In that case, the possibility of meaningfully praising the goodness of God would be lost.

The lesson here is that might does not make right, even if the might is the infinite might of God. To act morally is not to act out of fear of punishment, nor to act as one is commanded. Rather, it is to act as one ought to act, and how one ought to act is not dependent on anyone's power, even if the power be divine.

Thus actions are not right because God commands them; on the contrary, God commands them because they are right. What is right is independent of what God commands, for to be right, what God commands must conform to an independent standard.

We could act intentionally in accord with this standard without believing in the existence of God; therefore morality does not rest on that belief. Consequently those who do not believe in God can be highly moral (as well as immoral) people, and those who do believe in the existence of God can be highly immoral (as well as moral) people. This conclusion should come as no surprise to anyone who has contrasted the benevolent life of the Buddha, the inspiring teacher and an atheist, with the malevolent life of the monk Torquemada, who devised and enforced the boundless cruelties of the Spanish Inquisition.

In short, believing in the existence of God does not by itself imply any specific moral principles, and knowing God's will does not provide any justification for morality.

11

HEAVEN AND HELL

Even those who agree that morality stands independent of theism may harbor the thought that life on earth is followed by an afterlife in which good people abide forever in a place of joy, while others endure everlasting suffering in a place of doom. In other words, even if God doesn't create morality, God distributes rewards and punishments in accord with moral precepts. Doesn't that possibility provide a reason for adhering to ethical guidelines?

This line of thought does not even require confidence that God exists. Consider the reasoning offered by the French mathematician and philosopher Blaise Pascal. In his famous wager he argues that if you believe in God and God exists, then you attain heavenly bliss; if you believe in God and God doesn't exist, little is lost. On the other hand, if you don't believe in God and God exists, then you are doomed to the torments of damnation; if you don't believe in God and God doesn't exist, little is gained. Thus belief in God is the safest strategy.[1]

Pascal, however, failed to consider that a different kind of God might exist: for example, one who wishes us to hold only those beliefs supported by the available evidence. If such a God exists, then in the absence of evidence, *not* believing in God is the safest strategy.

Lacking knowledge about God, we do not even know whether God approves of any religious commitment. Perhaps God doesn't wish to be worshipped at public services or prayed to at times of hardship. Perhaps God rewards those who shun such activities. Indeed, God may favor those who meditate privately, if at all, and who, without appealing for God's help, display the fortitude to persevere in the face of difficulties. In that case avoiding ritual and prayer would be the wisest strategy. In sum, without more specific information about the intentions of God, all bets are off.

Yet many people, especially adherents to Christianity and Islam, may persist in believing in heaven and hell. Are these concepts viable?

They raise many puzzles. Why should finite wickedness deserve infinite punishment? Why should finite goodness deserve infinite reward? Is heaven reserved for adherents of only one religion? Are all other believers assigned to hell? What is the fate of those who lived before the development of any particular religion? Are they condemned to hell for not believing in a religion that had not yet been established? What about infants who die? How are they to be judged? What about beloved dogs, cats, and other creatures who have enriched the lives of so many persons? Might some of these animals merit a place in heaven? If not, how joyful can heaven be for those deprived of their faithful companions?

This last question is explored in "The Hunt," a provocative episode of the groundbreaking television series *The Twilight Zone*. An old hillbilly named Simpson and his hound dog, Rip, appear to drown in a backwoods pool. When they awaken the next morning, they are invisible to others, and soon Simpson realizes he and Rip have died. We then see them walk toward the local graveyard, come to an unfamiliar fence, follow it, and arrive at a gate. The gatekeeper explains to Simpson that he is at the entrance to heaven. He is welcome, but Rip is not; no dogs are allowed. Simpson becomes infuriated, declaring that he would rather stay with Rip than go to heaven, and man and dog walk away together. Soon they meet an angel sent to accompany them to heaven. Simpson protests that he won't go without Rip, and the angel tells Simpson that Rip is welcome in heaven. The angel explains that if Simpson had left Rip and gone through the gate, he would have made a terrible mistake. The gatekeeper had lied: the gate was the entrance to hell. Why had Rip been excluded? He would have smelled the brimstone and warned Simpson away. As the angel says, "You see, Mr. Simpson, a man, well, he'll walk right into Hell with both eyes open—but even the Devil can't fool a dog!"[2]

The effectiveness of this story depends in part on our being able to envision hell but not heaven. For when we realize that Simpson nearly made the mistake of going to hell, we can easily imagine the horrors that awaited him. We are all familiar with the nature of misery. Who among us has not known sorrow or suffering? Most have experienced anguish and agony. Too many have suffered tortures of mind and body, probably worse than any that could be found in hell.

Heaven, however, defies description. What events take place there? How do individuals relate to each other? What activities occupy them? A familiar supposition is that harps are played, but how long can harp music suffice for felicity? We understand the happiness that Rip brings Simpson, but how does it compare to the joys Simpson would experience in heaven? Not knowing, we are comfortable with Simpson rejecting heaven and staying with Rip.

To see additional difficulties involved in grasping the concept of heaven, consider the case of Willie Mays, the spectacular baseball player whose greatest joy was to play the game he loved. What does heaven offer him? Presumably bats, balls, and gloves are not found there, so what does Willie Mays do? Assuming he is the same person who made that spectacular catch in the 1954 World Series, how can the delights that supposedly await him in heaven match those he knew on Earth?

Furthermore, some of Mays's fans found great enjoyment in watching him play baseball. Won't they be denied this pleasure in heaven? Whatever heaven may offer them, they will miss watching Mays in action.

The problems mount. Consider two individuals, Leslie and Robin, and suppose that Leslie looks forward to spending eternity with Robin, whereas Robin looks forward to being forever free of Leslie. Assuming they retain their fundamental likes and dislikes, how can they both attain heavenly bliss?

More questions arise in attempting to understand the supposition that our bodies will be resurrected. Will they appear as they did when we were ten, forty, or seventy years old? If a person suffered from diabetes, will the resurrected body suffer from the disease? In what sense would a resurrected person be identical to the person who died? If a ship is destroyed and an identical one built, the second is different from the first. Similarly, if a person is destroyed and an identical one created, the second is different from the first.

One way to avoid these difficulties is to suppose that after death what survives are not bodies but souls. Thus although Simpson appeared to have a body, in essence he was only a soul. Was Rip also a soul, or do dogs not have souls? Can two souls inhabit a single body, or is the arrangement only one soul per person?

What, after all, is a soul? Supposedly, when added to a body, a soul converts that body into a person. Does the soul itself think and feel? In that case, it is already a person and needs no body. If it doesn't think and feel, how does it start doing so when it enters a body?

This problem can be avoided by recognizing that some bodies can think and feel. They do so as a result of possessing brains, which are physical objects and not immaterial souls. Yet brains cease functioning. People die.

Given all the bewildering questions that beset any attempt to provide a persuasive or even a coherent account of survival in a next world, we conclude that speculation about such obscure matters does not provide a reliable foundation for acting morally. If one is to be found, we need to look further.

12

MORAL JUDGMENTS

Some claim that just as we are subject to scientific laws, such as that water freezes at zero degrees centigrade and boils at one hundred degrees centigrade, so we are bound to acknowledge that murder is wrong and honesty is right. Moreover, just as laws of nature apply at any time and in any place, so do moral laws. The only difference is that laws of nature are tested by scientific method, while moral laws are tested by conscience. As the Scottish philosopher Thomas Reid writes, "Every man in his senses believes his eyes, his ears, and his other senses. . . . And he has the same reason, and, indeed, is under the same necessity of believing the clear and unbiased dictates of his conscience, with regard to which is honorable and what is base."[1]

This theory, however, runs into trouble. First, moral laws can be broken, whereas scientific laws cannot. A person can steal a book, thereby breaking a moral law, but cannot succeed in tossing a book in the air and prevent its being subject to the law of gravity. Second, the dictates of one person's conscience may conflict with those of another. How can we decide between them? We can appeal to the dictates of our own conscience, but ours may be biased. Or we can appeal to the dictates of the conscience of the majority, but theirs may also be mistaken. After all, moral principles are not decided by vote.

Perhaps, then, moral judgments aren't true or false but merely express preferences. Just as one person's favorite color may be blue while another's may be green, so one person favors honesty, another favors dishonesty. In that case reason offers no way to arbitrate the matter. Yet this view, too, is unsatisfactory, for we argue about moral issues, and the reasons we offer in defense of our views may lead others to change their minds, just as the reasons they offer in defense of their positions may lead us to alter ours. Thus reasoning plays a role in arriving at conclusions about matters of right and wrong.

Facing this impasse, we might make progress in understanding moral judgments if we consider first some value claims unrelated to ethics. For instance, we speak of "a good restaurant" or "the bad reception on your television." How are these statements justified?

Let's consider a specific example. Suppose you are a member of a softball league. Your friend Adam tells you that Seth is an excellent ballplayer, so you ask him to join your team, but he turns out to be woefully inadequate. He drops balls thrown to him, lets ground balls go through his legs, and strikes out almost every time he comes to bat. You tell Adam that his recommendation of Seth was a mistake. Either Adam does not know how to judge a good ballplayer, or someone has misled him about Seth's abilities, because obviously Seth is not a good ballplayer.

Notice that when you say that Seth is not a good ballplayer, you are neither appealing to the dictates of conscience nor expressing an arbitrary preference. Rather, you are basing your judgment on the facts—facts about softball, not facts about goodness. The reasons Seth is not a good ballplayer are that he hits poorly and fields inadequately. To defend your view, all you need do is point to Seth's batting and fielding averages. While disagreement may persist if Seth hits .250 and commits a few errors, without doubt a ballplayer who hits .150 and commits errors in every game is not a good ballplayer, whereas one who hits .350 and hardly ever commits an error is a good ballplayer. The distinction is clear, despite the possibility of borderline cases, just as the distinction between being bald and being hirsute is clear despite the possibility of disputable instances.

Note that if Seth hits and fields well, someone would be confused to wonder if Seth might still lack one attribute essential to a good ballplayer, namely goodness, because if Seth hits and fields well, then he is a good ballplayer. Goodness is not another attribute besides hitting and fielding well but a shorthand way of referring to those skills.

Suppose when you tell Adam that Seth is not a good ballplayer, Adam agrees that Seth doesn't hit or field well, but Adam argues that a good ballplayer is simply one who *looks* good when he plays, that is, someone who is attractive and graceful. He claims that because Seth has these attributes, he is a good ballplayer.

While Adam's reply would be exasperating, you could reply by emphasizing that the criteria of a good ballplayer are not arbitrary. You play softball to win; hence good players are those who help in winning. Seth doesn't do so and thus is not a good ballplayer.

If Adam thinks players who look good help the team win, his view can be disproven by an appeal to the record books. But if Adam believes softball is played not to win but to gain popularity, then players who look good may be more effective in achieving that aim. In that case, however, Adam's recommendations of ballplayers would be of no value to the overwhelming number of participants whose aim in playing the game is to score more runs than the opposition.

We have extended this example far enough to clarify the nature of non-moral value judgments. First, although the term "good" is a term of commendation, the criteria for its use vary depending on the context and our purposes. Good apples, good computers, and good ballplayers are good for different reasons. Second, if two people disagree about a value judgment but agree on the criteria for goodness, then their disagreement is in principle resolvable by the use of empirical testing procedures. Third, if two people disagree about a value judgment and also disagree on the criteria for goodness, then they need to consider why they have chosen their differing criteria. If they can find a basis for agreement on further ends that are supposed to justify the criteria, then their disagreement is again in principle resolvable by the use of empirical testing principles. If, however, their ends are fundamentally incompatible, then their disagreement will not yield to rational resolution.

These lessons apply not only to non-moral value judgments but also to moral ones. Hence what is meant by a good policy or action depends on the context and our purposes. If two people disagree about whether a policy or action is good but agree on the criteria for goodness, then their disagreement is in principle resolvable by the use of empirical testing procedures. If, however, their ends are fundamentally incompatible, then their disagreement will not yield to rational resolution.

An obvious question is: What are the chances that in a moral disagreement the disputants will agree on ends? At first glance, searching for consensus might appear hopeless, but it may be found by recognizing that we depend on others to achieve our most valued goals. As Jonathan Harrison observes, "We cannot conceive of a being like ourselves, who desires his own happiness, and the happiness of his family and friends (if not the happiness of the whole of mankind), who needs the company of his fellows, who is easily injured by their hostile acts, and who cannot continue to exist unless they co-operate with him—we cannot conceive of a being such as this approving of promise-breaking, dishonesty, and deliberate callousness to the interests of others."[2] In short, our humanity requires that we rely on others, and therefore we approve of actions that facilitate cooperation.

Any individual who rejects this way of thinking and instead favors persecution and cruelty for their own sake is not to be argued with but to be guarded against. Interestingly, no political leader has ever come to power by promising to increase hatred, violence, and oppression. Even the worst of dictators mouths the usual moral sentiments in order to gain popular support.

Thus if a moral skeptic should inquire why we should be concerned about the welfare of others, we can do no better than offer the response James Rachels provides: "The reason one ought not to do actions that would hurt other people is: other people would be hurt. The reason one ought to do actions that would benefit other people is: other people would be benefited." If such considerations count for nothing, then the discussion is over. But what if someone insistently maintains a position in favor of immorality? Then, quoting Rachels again, "he is saying something quite extraordinary. He is saying that he has no affection for friends or family, that he never feels pity or compassion, that he is the sort of person who can look on scenes of human misery with complete indifference, so long as he is not the one suffering. . . . Indeed, a man without any sympathy would scarcely be recognizable as a man."[3] The upshot is that a commitment to immorality is unlikely to be defended by anyone except an obstinate student in a philosophy seminar, who nevertheless expects to receive kind treatment and an equitable grade.

The claim has been made seriously, though, that all human actions are motivated by selfishness. According to this theory, known as "psychological egoism," all actions are attempts to enhance the agent's own pleasure. In other words, I am kind to others only to benefit myself.

An obvious response to this claim is to present cases in which people act unselfishly, such as a physician who lives among the poor to provide them with health care. The egoist responds, however, by asserting that the doctor derives pleasure from giving help and thus is acting selfishly after all.

The appropriate reply to this fallacious line of argument is provided by P. H. Nowell-Smith: "To be selfish is not to do what one wants to do or enjoys doing, but to be hostile or indifferent to the welfare of others."[4] In other words, an unselfish person cares about others, whereas a selfish person does not. Whether an action is selfish does not depend on whether someone wants to do it but on what that person wants to do. If the point is to assist others, then the action is unselfish.

Still one might ask why we should act unselfishly. Why not just appear to be moral rather than actually being moral? Why not follow the path of our old friend Fred?

Perhaps the best answer is provided by David Hume: "Knaves, with all their pretended cunning and abilities, [are] betrayed by their own maxims; and while they purpose to cheat with moderation and secrecy, a tempting incident occurs—nature is frail, and they give in to the snare, whence they can never extricate themselves without a total loss of reputation and the forfeiture of all future trust and confidence with mankind."[5] In brief, immoral action is always a threat to one's self-interest, and rarely can this threat be minimized sufficiently to render the risk rational.

But if, like Judah Rosenthal in *Crimes and Misdemeanors*, one decides to take a chance on unethical behavior, can we reason further with that individual? Perhaps nothing remains to be said except to recall the words of the French epigrammatist La Rochefoucauld: "To virtue's credit we must confess that our greatest misfortunes are brought about by vice."[6] Thus when sympathy is missing, morality rests solely on practicality.

13

MORAL STANDARDS

F ormulating ethical principles that would provide the answers to all moral problems is a daunting, perhaps impossible, task that in any case lies beyond our aims. Some thinkers, however, have supposed they could offer one supreme moral principle to serve as the ultimate ethical guide, requiring us to perform all the actions we ought to perform and forbidding us from performing all the actions we ought not perform. We doubt that any of these suggested principles is entirely successful. Without exploring any of them in depth, however, we shall raise difficulties with the most discussed proposals, thereby seeking a better understanding of the nature of acting morally, a necessary condition for living well.

One principle common to many religious traditions is the Golden Rule. Its positive formulation, attributed to Jesus, is: "In everything do to others as you would have them do to you."[1] The negative formulation, which appeared at least five centuries earlier, is attributed to Confucius and was later proposed by the Jewish sage Hillel. The latter puts it as follows:

"What is hateful to you, do not to your neighbor."[2] Is either of these the supreme moral principle?

Consider first the positive formulation. Granted, we usually should treat others as we would wish them to treat us. For instance, we should go to the aid of an injured person, just as we would wish that person to come to our aid if we were injured. If we always followed this rule, however, the results would be unfortunate. Masochists, for instance, derive pleasure from being hurt. Were they to act according to the principle in question, their duty would be to inflict pain, thereby doing to others as they wish done to themselves. Similarly, consider a person who enjoys receiving telephone calls, regardless of who is calling. The principle would require that person to telephone everyone, thereby reciprocating preferred treatment. Indeed, strictly speaking, to fulfill the positive formulation of the Golden Rule would be impossible, because we wish so many to do so much for us that we would not have time to do all that is necessary to treat them likewise. As Walter Kaufman commented, "anyone who tried to live up to Jesus' rule would become an insufferable nuisance."[3]

In this respect, the negative formulation of the Golden Rule is preferable, because it does not imply that we have innumerable duties toward everyone else. Neither does it imply that masochists ought to inflict pain on others, nor that those who enjoy receiving telephone calls ought themselves to make calls. While the negative formulation does not require these actions, however, neither does it forbid them. It enjoins us not to do to others what is hateful to ourselves, but pain is not hateful to the masochist and calls are not hateful to the telephone enthusiast. Thus, because the negative formulation does not prohibit actions that ought to be prohibited, it is not the supreme moral principle.

Let us next sketch two other standards of conduct, each of which has sometimes been thought to be the supreme moral principle. One was originally formulated by Immanuel Kant, who argues that the moral worth of an action is to be judged not by its consequences but by the nature of the maxim (the principle) that motivates the action. Right actions are not therefore necessarily those with favorable consequences but those performed from the duty of acting in accord with correct maxims. But which maxims are correct? According to Kant, only those that can serve as universal laws, because they are applicable without exception to every person at any time. In other words, you should act only on a maxim that can be universalized without contradiction.

To see what Kant has in mind, consider a specific example he uses to illustrate his view. Suppose you need to borrow money, but it will be lent to you only if you promise to pay it back. You realize, however, that you will not be able to honor the debt. Are you permitted to promise to repay the money, knowing you will not keep the promise? Kant proposes that the way to determine whether such an action is permissible is to universalize the maxim in question and see whether doing so leads to contradiction. The maxim is: "When I believe myself to be in need of money, I will borrow money and promise to repay it, although I know I shall never be able to do so." Can this maxim be universalized without contradiction? Kant argues that it cannot. "For the universality of a law which says that anyone who believes himself to be in need could promise what he pleased with the intention of not fulfilling it would make the promise itself and the end to be accomplished by it impossible; no one would believe what was promised to him but would only laugh at any such assertion as vain pretense."

In other words, to make promises with no intention of keeping them would lead to the destruction of the practice of promising. Thus, because the maxim in question cannot be universalized without contradiction, that maxim is not morally acceptable and, consequently, any action it motivates is immoral. According to Kant, then, the supreme moral principle is: "Act only according to that maxim by which you can at the same time will that it should become a universal law."[4]

This principle, unfortunately, prohibits actions that should be permitted. Although we might agree that the maxim of making insincere promises cannot be universalized, we can easily imagine cases in which a person ought to make a promise without any intention of keeping it. Suppose, for example, you and your family will starve to death unless you obtain food immediately, and a wealthy person offers to provide the food if you will promise repayment within twenty-four hours. Surely we would say, contrary to Kant's principle, under these circumstances you ought to act on a maxim that cannot be universalized and make a promise you have no intention of keeping.

Kant's insistence that proper maxims admit no exceptions leads him not only to disapprove actions that are appropriate but also to approve some that appear inconsistent. Maxims he sanctions may conflict, and in that case adherence to one involves the violation of another. In the preceding example, for instance, were you to act in accord with the maxim of never making insincere promises, you would violate another maxim affirmed by Kant, that of aiding those who are in distress. He argues that both maxims admit no exceptions, but because always abiding by both is impossible, Kant's position is problematic.

Perhaps his proposal raises difficulties because it concentrates exclusively on the reason for an action and fails to take into account its results. Thus let us next consider a principle that focuses on consequences, one defended by John Stuart Mill. He was a leading advocate for the ethical position known as "utilitarianism," according to which an action is right insofar as it promotes the happiness of humanity and wrong in so far as it promotes unhappiness. By the term "happiness" Mill means pleasure and the absence of pain. By "humanity" he means all persons, each valued equally. Thus Mill's supreme moral principle is: Act in such a way as to produce the greatest pleasure for the greatest number of people, each person's pleasure counting equally.

This principle avoids the pitfalls of Kant's view, for whereas he admitted no exceptions to moral rules and was thus led to condemn insincere promises that saved human lives, the utilitarian principle is flexible enough to allow for any exceptions that increase overall happiness. Although Mill would agree that insincere promises are usually wrong, because they are apt to cause more pain than pleasure, he would allow that in some cases, such as that of the starving family, an insincere promise is morally justifiable, as it would lead to greater overall happiness than any alternative.

The flexibility of the utilitarian principle is advantageous but also flawed, for it permits actions that should be prohibited. Consider, for example, inhabitants of a city who each week abduct a stranger and place the unfortunate person in an arena to wrestle a lion. When the inhabitants of the city are challenged to justify this practice, they reply that although one person suffers much pain, thousands of spectators obtain greater pleasure from this form of entertainment than from any other, so the spectacle is justified on utilitarian grounds. Clearly Mill's principle appears to yield an unacceptable implication. Other cases along similar lines likewise illustrate the laxity of utilitarianism. The sheriff who hangs an innocent person to satisfy the vengeance of the townspeople may maximize pleasure but nevertheless acts immorally. Also unethical is the teacher who awards all students A's to maximize their pleasure and avoid causing anyone pain.

One way to try to salvage the utilitarian principle is to argue that not all pleasures are of equal quality, that, for instance, the pleasure of spectators at a lion arena is less valuable than that enjoyed by those at a piano recital. As Mill writes, "It is better to be a human being dissatisfied than a pig satisfied; better to be Socrates dissatisfied than a fool satisfied. And if the fool, or the pig, are of a different opinion, it is because they only know their own side of the question. The other party to comparison knows both sides."[5]

This move is dubious. Some individuals, knowing both sides of the question, would prefer to witness a struggle between human and lion rather than between human and keyboard. Even if only one knowledgeable individual had such taste, why should that person's view be disregarded? Furthermore, Mill's principle cannot be salvaged by the claim that attendance at a piano recital develops sensitivity whereas a visit to a lion arena dulls it, for, according to utilitarianism, actions are good to the extent that they produce pleasure, not to the extent that they produce sensitivity.

Perhaps given the complexities of the human condition, any search for a supreme moral principle is doomed to failure, but the analysis so far, even while omitting innumerable clarifications, qualifications, and countermoves, has at least succeeded in calling attention to one fundamental feature of morality. The positive and negative formulations of the Golden Rule, the Kantian principle, and utilitarianism all serve as reminders that a moral person is obligated to be sensitive to others. This insight motivates not only the biblical injunction to treat our fellow human beings as we wish to be treated, but also the utilitarian insistence that each person's happiness is to count neither more nor less than another's. The same theme is central to Kant's view, a point he made explicit by claiming that the supreme moral principle could be reformulated as follows: "Act so that you treat humanity, whether in your own person or in that of another, always as an end and never as a means only."[6] In short, the moral point of view involves taking into account interests apart from our own.

With this insight in hand, let us recall the cases of Pat the philosopher and Lee the surfer. Both treat others with respect and hence act morally. Can we conclude, therefore, that they live well? Not necessarily. Suppose both are fundamentally frustrated or angry. Suppose they regret many decisions they have made, resent how they have been treated by others, or rue what they consider to be a long series of misfortunes. Under those circumstances, even if their actions have been ethical, for them the results would be negative.

The key question is: what missing element has to be added to an ethical life to render it well-lived? We propose as the answer: happiness.

14

CHOOSING THE EXPERIENCE MACHINE

A central issue about happiness is whether its value depends on how it is achieved. Suppose someone could be made happy by having illusory experiences. Would anyone welcome that possibility?

This question lies at the heart of a frequently cited and widely admired thought experiment offered by Robert Nozick. He conceives the following hypothetical situation: "Suppose there were an experience machine that would give you any experience you desired. Superduper neuropsychologists could stimulate your brain so that you would think and feel you were writing a great novel, or making a friend, or reading an interesting book. All the time you would be floating in a tank, with electrodes attached to your brain. . . . Would you plug in?"

Nozick presumes that no one would choose this option and offers three reasons. First, "we want to *do* certain things, and not just have the experience of doing them." Second, "we want to *be* a certain way, to be a certain sort of person." Third, "plugging in . . . limits us to a man-made reality." He concludes that because we would not use an experience machine "something matters to us in addition to experience."[1]

In the decades since Nozick posed this puzzle and presented his solution, virtually all philosophers have taken his treatment as conclusive. Almost no one has argued that people would choose the experience machine.[2]

To find such unanimity is unexpected, but the situation is especially surprising because Nozick's conclusion appears mistaken. In support of this view, we shall offer various reasons why an individual might be inclined to choose the experience machine. We illustrate these by the use of examples at least as plausible as the experience machine itself.

First, consider cases in which people may not desire to *do* certain things but instead want to have the experience of doing them. For example, one of the pleasures of going to the movies is having the opportunity to experience adventures we would not risk in reality. While safe in our plush seats, we can feel the excitement of skiing precipitously down a steep mountain, participating in dangerous international intrigue, or battling a typhoon. Yet how many of us actually wish to *do* any of these things?[3] Such cases demonstrate that using an experience machine is not in principle objectionable. The only controversial issue is the length of time for which you would be willing to employ it.

The cinema, however, is not the only case in which we seek appearance rather than reality. Consider the popularity of bungee jumping, roller coasters, aggressive computer games, or reenactments of Civil War battles. All these activities offer participants the experience of pursuing thrilling adventures without facing the possible consequences of the real-life activities they simulate.

Another sort of escape from reality is offered by psychedelic drugs. Nozick notes that these are viewed by some "as mere local experience machines," but he does not draw the inference that their widespread use suggests that many would welcome the opportunity not only to drop out but also to plug in.[4] A similar point could be made about the widespread use of alcohol to distort reality.[5]

Granted, the examples we have discussed so far involve individuals who might use the machine only occasionally. And in a later discussion Nozick reformulates his challenge: "The question is not whether to try the machine temporarily, but whether to enter it for the rest of your life."[6]

In response, let us turn to cases in which people, to change who they are, might choose the experience machine for the rest of their lives. Consider golf enthusiasts who struggle to master this most intractable of games. Doing so at a professional level necessitates spending innumerable hours hitting thousands of golf balls day after day over a period of at least a decade. Not many of us would choose to spend our lives in such tiresome training (even if we had the needed ability to excel, as most of us do not). Suppose, however, that without any preparation you could experience hitting massive drives, pinpoint iron shots, and precision putts, all while hearing the roars of the crowd as you win major championships. Wouldn't many amateur golfers want that life? Wouldn't they be willing to trade their frustration on the fairways for a lifetime of golfing triumphs?

Or consider the ardent music lover who dreams of becoming a concert violinist. Few persons, even if they had the necessary talent, would choose to exhaust their energy and patience in such a strenuous effort. Suppose, though, that without any exertion they could have the experience of performing recitals in great halls and appearing as soloist with the world's leading symphony orchestras, each time receiving adulation from a cheering audience. Might some not be willing to trade their lives to undergo such experiences?

Imagine that instead of living your own life, you could choose to live the life of Alexander the Great, Cleopatra, or Babe Ruth. Do you suppose no one willingly would make that trade, even though the experience machine could be programmed to omit a life's tribulations and focus on its triumphs? Or perhaps you prefer the cinematic adventures of Clark Gable, Katharine Hepburn or Humphrey Bogart. Would no one choose those? How about living the life of secret agent James Bond? Wouldn't that option tempt some?

Another sort of case concerns individuals who would wish to change their characters. For example, how would you feel if you possessed the moral and intellectual virtues of the Buddha? The experience machine could provide the answer.

Or suppose you wish to have been present at the trial of Socrates, the Lincoln-Douglas debates, or the riot at the Paris premiere of Stravinsky's *Le Sacre du printemps*. The experience machine could make you a spectator at those events. Of course, you wouldn't actually be there. Your experience, however, would be indistinguishable from reality.

The experience machine would also enable you to have experiences of inestimable personal value. For example, you could experience a world inhabited by your loved ones who have died. In our dreams we often imagine such a scenario and, when awakened, are disappointed that the dream did not continue. Suppose, however, you could opt for the vision to endure. Wouldn't many do so?

Or imagine living again in the time and place of your younger days. Such is the plot of "Walking Distance," an early episode of *The Twilight Zone* written by the program's creator, Rod Serling, with evocative music by the famed composer Bernard Hermann.[7] Considered by many the finest show of the entire series, this nostalgic story captures the poignant tale of world-weary advertising executive Martin Sloan, who returns to his hometown only to find it exactly as it was at the time of his youth. He confronts his parents, who believe he is a lunatic, and tries to converse with himself as a child, but the frightened boy runs away. Martin, though, cannot remain there. As his father, who at last understands the situation, insists, "only one summer to every customer." In a moving voice-over at the conclusion, Serling observes,

Martin Sloan, age thirty-six, vice president in charge of media. Successful in most things, but not in the one effort that all men try at some time in their lives—trying to go home again. And also like all men perhaps there'll be an occasion—maybe a summer night sometime—when he'll look up from what he's doing and listen to the distant music of a calliope, and hear the voices and the laughter of his past. And perhaps across his mind there'll flit a little errant wish, that a man might not have to become old, never outgrow the parks and the merry-go-rounds of his youth. And he'll smile then too because he'll know it is just an errant wish, some wisp of memory not too important really, some laughing ghosts that cross a man's mind.[8]

But the experience machine could fulfill that wish. Would no one choose to do so?

Let us return to the present and recognize another reason why people might choose the experience machine: a desire to escape a life of sorrow or even agony. Nozick, when revisiting the idea of the experience machine, declares such cases irrelevant, perhaps because he presumes that they occur infrequently.[9] The truth, however, is otherwise. The plight of so many unfortunate people is captured in this verse of William Blake:

Every Night & every Morn
Some to Misery are Born.
Every Morn & every Night
Some are Born to sweet delight.
Some are Born to sweet delight,
Some are Born to Endless Night.[10]

Those born in the latter circumstances would surely choose the delights of the experience machine in place of their dreadful lives on earth.

How many unfortunates are in this position? Consider Schopenhauer's view: "Life with its hourly, daily, weekly, yearly, little, greater, and great misfortunes, with its deluded hopes and its accidents destroying all our calculations, bears so distinctly the impression of something with which we must become disgusted, that it is hard to conceive how one has been able to mistake this and allow oneself to be persuaded that life is there in order to be thankfully enjoyed, and that man exists in order to be happy."[11]

One need not be as pessimistic as Schopenhauer to sympathize with his outlook. If the experience machine offers joys in place of tortures of mind and body, the burden of argument would surely rest on those who would urge against its use.

After all, we evade the pain of surgery by the use of anesthesia; we thereby avoid reality. If one's life itself is little more than a succession of pains, why not opt for the delights of the experience machine?

Nozick asserts that "plugging into the machine is a kind of suicide." He says, however, that the machine enables one to choose a "lifetime of bliss." Hence wouldn't plugging in be the closest we could come to heaven on earth? After all, what is heaven supposed to be if not eternal bliss?

Nozick concludes that we desire to be "in contact with reality."[12] Knowing what we do of reality, though, why assume that remaining in touch with it is invariably preferable to a lifetime of bliss?

The array of cases we have presented demonstrates the implausibility of the assumption that no one would use the experience machine. Indeed, were such a machine on the market, a smart investor would seek to purchase it, or at least buy stock in the company that manufactured it.

But what lessons are we supposed to learn from the claim that no one would choose the machine? Jonathan Glover believes Nozick's thought experiment demonstrates that "we care about more than our own experience."[13] No doubt some do, and some don't. We shouldn't, however, confuse caring about something with being unwilling to trade it under appropriate circumstances. Epidural anesthesia is chosen by many women to ease the pain of labor and delivery, but doing so does not imply that they devalue the reality of childbirth. Similarly, choosing to plug into the experience machine does not imply a lack of concern for reality. Such concern may simply be overridden.

James Griffin presumes that rejecting the experience machine demonstrates that knowing the truth rather than being comforted by delusions makes for "a better life."[14] That conclusion is easier to reach, however, if one's life is deeply satisfying. But for those suffering in "endless night," the value of delusions should not be so quickly dismissed. In any case, would you want to know the truth regarding the time and circumstances of your death? Indeed, grasping more of the truth does not always lead to a better life. Who would wish to discern the deepest thoughts of all others? The truth matters but it may be traded for something more valuable.

We don't doubt that some people would prefer reality to the experience machine. Does that supposition imply, as L. W. Sumner claims, that "being in touch with reality makes for a better life"?[15] The conclusion doesn't follow unless we assume that following one's preferences always leads to a better life. Yet while some of our choices are wise, others are not. Whether we choose to plug into the experience machine does not prove the good sense of doing so.

Nozick believes that we value reality over the mere experience of it. As our cases demonstrate, though, sometimes we don't value reality highly or even at all. As David Hume in his *Dialogues Concerning Natural Religion* puts the point in the mouth of the orthodox believer Demea: "The whole earth . . . is cursed and polluted. A perpetual war is kindled amongst all living creatures. Necessity, hunger, want, stimulate the strong and courageous; Fear, anxiety, terror agitate the weak and infirm. The first entrance into life gives anguish to the new-born infant and to its wretched parent; Weakness, impotence, distress, attend each stage of that life; And it is at last finished in agony and horror."[16]

Such is our world, and for good reason some would wish to explore other possibilities. They may still value aspects of reality but would be willing to trade them for something they believe more valuable. Whether such exchanges would be wise depends on the circumstances. To suppose, however, that regardless of the attractiveness of the alternatives such a choice would never be made is unwarranted. Once that error is recognized, Nozick's experience machine can be seen as what it is: a dream many may yearn for, but not evidence that mere experience is insufficient for happiness.

15

HAPPINESS AND IGNORANCE

I f happiness can be found in the illusions created by the experience machine, can happiness also be based on ignorance? Some suppose not, but we disagree. Consider the following case based on actual events.

Eve is an assistant professor at Euclid University. She is happy, enjoying the campus setting, amiable colleagues, and motivated students. She is especially pleased with the head of her department, a renowned scholar who is highly complimentary about her. The head asks her to serve on important committees, represent the department in college-wide activities, and lead in planning the department's curriculum. She is delighted to participate in these undertakings, while she continues to relish her teaching and develop her research.

In her sixth year at Euclid, Eve is considered for tenure. She assumes all will go smoothly, especially because she has such strong support from the departmental head. She recognizes, though, that her scholarship presents a problem. She has spent so much time undertaking departmental responsibilities that she has published only a couple of articles. Yet she is confident of a positive outcome because her efforts have greatly benefitted the department and the university.

But matters go awry. In view of her thin publication record, the department recommends against her receiving tenure. The head does not support her, writing that although her service has been useful, she has not demonstrated strong potential as a scholar. When Eve is rejected for tenure and thwarted in her repeated attempts to obtain another faculty position, she is forced to leave academic life. She is furious at the departmental head, disappointed with her colleagues, and extraordinarily unhappy.

Such a chain of events is not unusual. While this tale offers lessons about academic ethics (which we shall here omit),[1] it also has implications for understanding happiness.

First, for years Eve was happy at Euclid. She did not realize that the departmental head's praise was insincere, so she enjoyed their interaction. Had she known how the head actually judged her, she would have been unhappy. She didn't know, though, and thus was happy.

Richard Kraut disagrees with this description of such a case. He argues that whether a person is living happily depends on whether that individual is "attaining the important things he values, or if he comes reasonably close to this high standard."[2] Because Eve was deceived, believing she was making progress toward attaining tenure when she wasn't, Kraut would claim she was not happy.

This way of understanding the situation, however, is unpersuasive. Eve went to school each day pleased with the ambience, the faculty, the students, and the work. Hence she was happy. Granted, her outlook eventually changed, and her happiness disappeared, but her later unhappiness doesn't change her earlier happiness. Future events cannot alter past ones.

Admittedly, her past happiness was based on misreading the situation, for she didn't understand the trouble she faced. Had she realized, she wouldn't have been happy and might have sought to leave Euclid. But she didn't want to leave. Why not? Because she was happy.

So much for the claim that happiness depends on knowing the truth. Yet Eve's story also clarifies another aspect of happiness.

Note that Eve's reports of her initial happiness and later unhappiness were uncontestable. If during Eve's earlier years at Euclid someone had told her that she wasn't happy, perhaps because Euclid's faculty wasn't as friendly as she supposed, or other schools had better students than Euclid, or a different career path was preferable to that of a professor, none of these claims, even if true, would have proven that Eve wasn't happy. Perhaps other people wouldn't have been happy in her situation, but their preferences were irrelevant to her outlook. If she asserted sincerely that she was happy, then she was.

On the other hand, when she realized the treachery of the head and became indignant, no one could disprove that she was unhappy. Imagine Eve's going to the dean's office to complain about the tenure decision and express her unhappiness. Suppose the dean had replied, "You're wrong. You're not unhappy. You're just confused. You think you're unhappy, but you're not." Deans have said foolish things, but this reply would top them all. If Eve asserted she was unhappy, then she was.

Perhaps this point was never made more forcefully than in Edwin Arlington Robinson's poignant poem "Richard Cory":

Whenever Richard Cory went down town,
We people on the pavement looked at him.
He was a gentleman from sole to crown,
Clean favored, and imperially slim.

And he was always quietly arrayed,
And he was always human when he talked;
But still he fluttered pulses when he said,
"Good-morning," and he glittered when he walked.

And he was rich—yes, richer than a king—
And admirably schooled in every grace:
In fine, we thought that he was everything
To make us wish that we were in his place.

So on we worked, and waited for the light,
And went without the meat, and cursed the bread;
And Richard Cory, one calm summer night,
Went home and put a bullet through his head.[3]

Whether Richard Cory was unhappy was up to him, not anyone else. Similarly, our reports of our own happiness or unhappiness are definitive. Of course, over time they may change. At first Eve was happy at Euclid, but when she left she was miserable. Suppose, however, she refused to give up her ambition for a successful career and decided to enter law school. Three years later she graduated with honors, then became an associate in a large law firm, eventually earning more than Euclid's president. Along the way, she realized that she preferred interacting with corporate clients rather than late adolescents. Now she is happy again.

Such changes are unsurprising, because as events occur, our outlook may alter. Happiness may turn to unhappiness, or vice versa.

One final point. Eve's happiness does not depend on whether college teaching or legal work is more meaningful. Recall Susan Wolf's doubts about the significance of a life single-mindedly given to corporate law. Eve has no such doubts, although she may question the significance of a life single-mindedly given to academic affairs. Whether an enterprise makes you happy, however, depends on you, not on what most people believe or what a philosopher theorizes. The decision is personal.

16

ASSESSING ACHIEVEMENT

Before leaving the story of Eve, let us revisit it with one change. Again she is denied tenure, embarks on a career in the law, and achieves major success. This time, though, her anger at the departmental head, her former colleagues, and the administration of Euclid University never subsides. Indignation permeates her outlook ever after.

The only difference from the original account lies in Eve's attitude. Her accomplishments remain the same. Yet in this case most people would say that her life has not been well-lived, because it has been ruined by her reaction to events.

This point is crucial, so let us see the same principle exemplified in an entirely different setting. Imagine two swimmers, Sandy and Terry, who compete in the Olympics. Sandy wins a silver medal, while Terry finishes last. Thus Sandy is successful and Terry is not. But if Sandy looks back at the experience with disappointment because of failure to win a gold medal, whereas Terry is delighted merely to have competed, then whose experience was the more fulfilling? Surely Terry's, for while fond memories of the Games will forever warm Terry's life, Sandy will find cold comfort by focusing exclusively on missing the gold.

To understand living well, you need to distinguish between a person's achievements and that individual's assessment of those achievements. Emphasizing this distinction goes back in the history of ideas most famously to the Greek thinker Epicurus (341–270 B.C.E.), who was about twenty years old when Aristotle died. Epicurus founded a philosophical community in Athens called "the Garden," in which, remarkably for the time, men and women as well as free persons and slaves participated on equal terms. He was a prolific author, but unfortunately few of his writings survive.

Before examining several of his most crucial ideas that shed light on our subject, a brief overview of his thought is in order. Epicurus stresses that the gods are detached from us. They exist, but we are not their concern nor they ours. The fundamental structure of the world is that of atoms in motion, although persons have free will as a result of uncaused swerves in the atoms. Our knowledge is derived from sense experience. The ultimate aim of philosophy is to provide a guide to living well, maximizing pleasures and minimizing pains, but accepting such pains as lead to greater pleasures and rejecting such pleasures as lead to greater pains. The result is a tranquil life that avoids extravagance. Virtues such as temperance or courage are prized, because they lead to pleasure. So do friendships, which are therefore to be cultivated. Death is not to be feared, because while we exist, death is not present; when death is present, we are not. Our lives on earth are not followed by any afterlife.

Central to Epicurus's thought is the distinction between a successful life and a satisfying life. As Julia Annas explains the view of Epicurus, "happiness is not to be identified with the course of our life as a whole, but with the inner attitude the agent has to that extended course, an attitude that is not dependent on the way that course goes on. Thus being happy is consistent with the collapse or reversal of the outward course of one's life, and it is not curtailed when the course of one's life is curtailed."[1]

Our tendency is to judge a life by a person's achievements, whether in terms of fame, wealth, or a variety of other accomplishments. By that criterion, the well-known person has lived more successfully than the obscure person, the rich person has lived more successfully than the poor one, and the academic who has published numerous books and articles has lived more successfully than one who has published little. This way of thinking leads to viewing life as a game, in which the winners and losers are decided by who at the end has more fame, more money, or, in academia, a more impressive curriculum vitae.

None of these accomplishments, however, is a sign of having lived well. To suppose so is to commit what we might call "the Richard Cory fallacy," mistakenly reasoning that success implies satisfaction. Epicurus recognizes this error: "He who has learned the limits of life knows that that which removes the pain due to want and makes the whole of life complete is easy to obtain; so that there is no need of actions which involve competition."[2] In short, life is not a contest. Anyone, regardless of wealth or fame, can obtain the contentment crucial to living well. The key is seeking pleasure with prudence.

17

PLEASURES AND PAINS

While Epicurus believes that happiness is found in pleasure, his understanding of pleasure is atypical, for he associates the pleasant life with tranquility achieved through limiting desires and avoiding fears. The outlook of Epicurus should not conjure up images of carousers at an endless banquet, consuming copious amounts of food and spirits. Rather, his understanding of hedonism calls for restraint, resulting in freedom from all suffering, whether mental or physical. To reiterate, not all pleasures should be pursued nor all pains avoided, for some pleasures lead to much pain while some pains lead to much pleasure. As he says, "sometimes we pass over many pleasures, when greater discomfort accrues to us as the result of them: and similarly we think many pains better than pleasures, since a greater pleasure comes to us when we have endured pains for a long time."[1]

Central to the outlook of Epicurus is recognizing the interdependence of pleasures and pains. To put the point generally, our choices have consequences, both advantageous and disadvantageous, and in deciding what course to follow we need to consider as many of them as possible. Do some choices have only good consequences and others only bad ones? Thinking so is a mistake, a failure to recognize a critical aspect of the human condition.

This lesson was highlighted many years ago for one of this book's coauthors, Steven M. Cahn, when he and his wife sought to buy a house. They asked acquaintances to recommend a real estate agent, and one name, Jeff Bell, was mentioned repeatedly. Therefore they called him to ask if he would assist them. As they later discovered, he usually dealt with houses in a much higher price range than they could afford, but, as a favor to mutual friends, he agreed to help.

Soon the Cahns understood why he was so highly regarded. He never pretended that any property, no matter how attractive, was without drawbacks. In case these were being overlooked, he would patiently enumerate them, so that his clients, even if enamored with a place, would fully understand its disadvantages. Nor would he dismiss any property, no matter how unappealing, without calling attention to its advantages. In every case, he would conclude his assessment with words that the Cahns came to consider his motto: "It's a trade-off." Eventually his skill in negotiation led to their acquiring at a reasonable price a home that met their needs. Was it a trade-off? Of course, yet the plusses outweighed the minuses.

As the Cahns once told Jeff, his words pointed to an important truth that transcended real estate: every choice in life is a trade-off. They promised him that someday his saying would appear in print. Sadly, he is no longer alive, but his insight deserves to be heeded.

Wherever you reside, your location has certain advantages and disadvantages. It's a trade-off. Wherever you go to school, that institution offers certain advantages and disadvantages. It's a trade-off. Whatever your career choice, it has certain advantages and disadvantages. Again, it's a trade-off.

Once you grasp this essential feature of life, you stop seeking options that have positive consequences but no negative ones. The question to ask in any situation is: what are the negative consequences of the choice I find most attractive? If you can't accept those consequences, then you need to make a different choice. If you are unable to think of any negative consequences, you haven't pondered the matter deeply enough. As Epicurus writes, "Every desire must be confronted with this question: what will happen to me, if the object of my desire is accomplished and what if it is not?"[2] Whether to act on any particular desire depends on the answer to that question.

Attaining challenging goals will require that you undertake work you would prefer to avoid. In whatever activity you seek to excel, whether athletics, business, scholarship, or some other pursuit, the path is difficult because achieving the pleasure involves enduring much pain.

That lesson is exemplified in the following true story of a boy named Bobby, who attended a summer sports camp where his superb skills were apparent to all. He was only fifteen, but his prowess was remarkable, and because baseball was the game he loved, everyone assumed he would one day be a major league star.

For many years after, however, most at the camp heard nothing about him. Then one summer day, when former campers were invited to visit, he appeared and participated in a ballgame. Although still outstanding, he had gained weight and slowed down considerably. Later he reported that he had played briefly in the minor leagues but had soon given up baseball and become a construction worker. His voice was quiet, as of one whose dream had long since faded.

When a veteran counselor who had known Bobby all his life was asked how such a superb athlete could have failed, this was the response: "Sure, he loved to play baseball, but that's all he would do—play it. He wasn't willing to work at it. Fielding ground balls at training camp may be fun for a while, but as the hours pass the fun disappears. The strain begins to tell, and the field empties. Before long just a few hopefuls are still practicing. They're the only ones with a real chance to make the majors. The rest better find something else to do."

Possibly Bobby found satisfaction in his life without ever playing in the major leagues; in that case, assuming he acted ethically, he lived well. But in calculating which pleasures to pursue, he needed to realize that they came at a price. If he wasn't willing to pay it, then he wouldn't be able to obtain those pleasures.

The same lesson is found in mastering any substantial subject, for each presents obstacles. As Alfred North Whitehead observes: "To write poetry you must study metre; and to build bridges you must be learned in the strength of material. Even the Hebrew prophets had learned to write, probably in those days requiring no mean effort. The untutored art of genius is—in the words of the Prayer Book—a vain thing, fondly invented."[3]

Acquiring an education is not sheer joy. It involves careful study, a concern for detail, and the fortitude to carry projects through to completion regardless of their appeal. Any supposed royal road to learning is no more than a shortcut to ignorance. In short: no pain, no pleasure.

Epicurus teaches that happiness is within our power, but we need to make prudent choices after careful consideration of the range of consequences. As he puts it, "Every pleasure then because of its natural kinship to us is good, yet not every pleasure is to be chosen: even as every pain also is an evil, yet not all are always of a nature to be avoided. Yet by a scale of comparison and by the consideration of advantages and disadvantages we must form our judgment on all these matters. For the good on certain occasions we treat as bad, and conversely the bad as good."[4]

The last sentence captures the essence of the view of Epicurus. The good, that is, pleasure, is sometimes bad for us, while the bad, that is, pain, is sometimes good for us. Making wise judgments about good and bad is prudence.

18

FEAR OF THE DIVINE

Epicurus believes that unnecessary fears are the main source of unhappiness. Hence ridding oneself of them is key to living a satisfying life. He focuses on three sources of fear: fear of the divine, fear of unfulfilled desires, and fear of death. Let us consider each in turn.

As to fear of the divine, note that Epicurus is primarily concerned with plural gods. The analysis he offers, however, is equally applicable to a monotheistic perspective, and to emphasize this point we shall refer to the focus of his thinking as "God."

The existence of God is not for Epicurus a matter of dispute, given its wide acceptance as an item of knowledge. But why should we fear God, given that our experience does not extend beyond the natural world?

Many suppose that a reason for concern is that God rewards the good and punishes the wicked. As Epicurus observes, however, this claim is not borne out by the available evidence. That "the greatest misfortunes befall the wicked and the greatest blessings the good" are "false suppositions."[1] How do believers reply when confronted by this challenge? They are inclined to deny that we understand God. Such an approach, for instance, is taken by many commentators on the Book of Job. Their response to God's unsavory bet with Satan is to deny that we comprehend God's purposes.

For example, "the Book of Job teaches us that God's ways are beyond the complete understanding of our little minds. Like Job, we must believe that God, who placed us in this world, knows what is best for us. Such faith in the goodness of God, even though we cannot altogether understand it, brings us strength and confidence to face our calamities, and sorrows and sufferings."[2]

Here's another instance: "The total mystery of God can be gleaned from the Book of Job. . . . [Job] cannot any longer allow himself to think of God as just or unjust, at least as these terms are understood by man. These categories have no meaning when applied to God."[3]

The problem, however, is that if words do not have their ordinary meaning when applied to God, what do they mean? For example, if God's knowledge has nothing in common with human knowledge, then, as the medieval Jewish philosopher Levi ben Gershom (Gersonides) argues, we might as well say that God *lacks* knowledge, adding the proviso that the term "knowledge" applied to God does not have the same meaning as it does ordinarily. In other words, once we allow ourselves to use terms without being able to offer any explanation of them, we might as well say anything at all, for none of what we say makes any sense.

Suppose, though, we use words with their ordinary meaning. Then we face the problem of evil, which in the following succinct formulation Hume attributes to Epicurus: "Is he [God] willing to prevent evil but not able? then he is impotent. Is he able, but not willing? then he is malevolent. Is he both able and willing? Whence then is evil?"[4]

One popular response to this challenge is to take refuge in the claim that God is unknowable. But this admission undermines the impact of the theistic position. To see why, suppose we reduce theism to its least controversial version, one that Hume in his *Dialogues Concerning Natural Religion* attributes to Philo the skeptic: "*the cause or causes of order in the universe probably bear some remote analogy to human intelligence.*" Given, however, the vagueness introduced by the phrases "cause or causes," "probably," and "remote analogy," the theistic position is robbed of significance. We are left only with Philo's observation that theism so understood "affords no inference that affects human life."[5]

This view is the one Epicurus espouses, when he says that "the impious man is not he who denies the gods of the many, but he who attaches to the gods the beliefs of the many."[6] For if the theistic beliefs of the many are not true, if God is not properly described as just or unjust and if God exceeds human understanding, then why should divine matters be a source of anxiety?

You might as well tremble at a possible threat from a snark.[7] What is a snark? It's nature is incomprehensible. Why, then, be frightened of it? Someone who dreads a snark but grasps nothing about any impact it has on us is unnecessarily concerned. Epicurus would say the same about anyone who fears the divine.

A near contemporary of Epicurus, living far away, adopts a similar approach. His name is Xunzi (pronounced "shun-see"), a Confucian scholar of the third century B.C.E. He considers any belief in supernaturalism to be pointless because whatever "Heaven" may be, it is not concerned with human action and provides no rewards or punishments. Rites are not appeals to otherworldly forces but human inventions that ornament social life and serve as expressions of emotion. In his view, "You pray for rain and it rains. Why? For no particular reason, I say. It is just as though you had not prayed for rain and it rained anyhow."[8] Xunzi's rationalism strongly influenced the later development of Confucianism.

Many centuries later in the West, a similar position is held by those who are known as "deists." They affirm the existence of God but find formal religion superfluous and deny all claims to supernatural revelation, thus providing no reason to look to the divine as a source of help or hindrance. Among the deists are Voltaire, Jean Jacques Rousseau, Benjamin Franklin, George Washington, and Thomas Jefferson, an estimable group indeed.

In sum, to the extent Epicurus contemplates deities, he thinks of them, in D. S. Hutchinson's words, as "in a state of bliss, unconcerned about anything, without needs, invulnerable to any harm, and generally living an enviable life."[9] While we may pray to the divine, sacrifice to the divine, or worship the divine, the divine remains unconcerned about us. Why, then, be afraid?

FEAR OF UNFULFILLED DESIRES

A second source of fear is the concern that we may fail to achieve our desires. If these are what Epicurus calls "natural and necessary," such as wanting food, water, and shelter, then they are limited in scope and relatively easy to obtain. Doing so should not involve excessive trouble.[1]

They might, of course, be fulfilled in luxurious ways, such as eating expensive food, drinking water from a silver goblet, or living in an elegant home. Epicurus describes these as "natural but non-necessary" desires, and he allows that these preferences may be indulged but always with care, so that they do not bring with them unwanted pains.

Our remaining desires are, according to Epicurus, "due to idle imaginings."[2] These include the quest for wealth, power, and fame—precisely the goals of the aforementioned Fred. These have no limit; they stretch on "to infinity."[3] Those who crave them are never satisfied. Seekers of wealth always want more wealth; seekers of power always want more power; seekers of fame always want more fame.

Epicurus warns against these desires because almost invariably the attempts to fulfill them carry unwanted costs.

He would anticipate that someone like Fred will eventually fall prey to unhappiness, undone by insatiable appetites. Seeing others who are more wealthy, more powerful, and more famous, Fred will try even harder to outdo them, leading to increased recklessness and ultimate failure.

Casinos, for instance, depend on winners not walking away but continuing to play, seeking to enhance their take. The longer they stay, the greater the odds they will leave as losers.

For one who holds power, relinquishing it is rarely voluntary. Perhaps the most notable exception was George Washington, who could have been president as long as he lived but chose to retire after completing two terms. The significance of his action was well captured by the eminent historian Gordon S. Wood, who wrote: "Washington's most important act as president was giving up the office. The significance of his retirement from the presidency is easily overlooked today, but his contemporaries knew what it meant. . . . That the chief executive of a state should willingly relinquish his office was an objective lesson in republicanism at a time when the republican experiment throughout the Atlantic world was very much in doubt."[4]

Washington, of course, was a rarity, so Epicurus's concern about the desire for power remains acute. Those who crave it, by enhancing their efforts to hold on to it, increase the chances that their quest will lead to immorality or illegality. The sizable number of office-holders in the United States who end up in court or prison would come as no surprise to Epicurus.

Those who desire fame, like those who seek riches and power, are driven by an unquenchable urge that some eventually realize is harmful to themselves. This lesson is offered at the end of Plato's *Republic*, a work Epicurus would have known, when Plato tells the myth of Er, the story of a valiant man who died but came back to life two days later and reported what he had seen in the next world. There he found that souls were permitted to select their future lives. The last choice fell to the soul of Odysseus, "whose ambition was so abated by memory of his former labors that he went about for a long time looking for a life of quiet obscurity. When at last he found it lying somewhere rejected by all the rest, he chose it gladly, saying that he would have done the same if his lot had come first."[5]

Celebrity is ephemeral. Those seeking to achieve it from favorable media coverage soon learn that what the media gives, it can take away. Similarly, if your aim as a writer is to achieve renown, then you are apt to be disappointed because even in the rare instance in which a specific work is celebrated, the author as an individual personality will almost surely be forgotten. Such is also the fate of those who devote themselves to the success of an organization. Their contributions, however valuable, are not apt to be long remembered.

We reflect on this phenomenon each time we come to the landmark building in midtown Manhattan that is now the home of the City University of New York Graduate Center, founded in 1961. The library is named for mathematician Mina Rees, the school's first president, whose commitment to the highest academic standards set the tone for the future success of the institution. After serving a decade as its head, she was succeeded by psychologist Harold M. Proshansky, for whom the auditorium is named. His fortitude sustained the school throughout its next two decades, while its existence was threatened repeatedly by cuts in state budgets. Although students regularly use the library and attend events in the auditorium, when they are asked to identify the individuals in whose honor the library and auditorium are named, few know, and not too many care. So much for lasting fame.

Rather than seeking ways to satisfy desires that flow from "idle imaginings," the aim should be to try to reduce or eliminate them. As Epicurus writes, "If you wish to make Pythocles rich, do not give him more money but diminish his desire."[6]

But can individuals alter their desires? They can, and the ability to do so is a source of tremendous personal power. The overeater can eat in a healthier manner. The person in poor physical condition can exercise. The individual who is not doing well in school can study more intensely. More pointedly, one who has sought to acquire as much wealth as possible can instead focus on philanthropy, while another who has chased after fame can become dedicated to avoiding the spotlight while still showing concern for others. The self-control required to achieve such results is sometimes referred to as "self-discipline," felicitously described by John Dewey as "power at command . . . a power to endure in an intelligently chosen course in face of distraction, confusion, and difficulty."[7]

How is such power acquired? The answer, provided in Aristotle's *Nicomachean Ethics*,[8] is that repeated acts of self-control result in a self-controlled person who not only performs self-controlled actions but does so from a fixed character. Thus even a single act of self-control can begin the development of a habit of self-control. The most effective approach is not, for example, to resolve to exercise every day for the next year; instead, exercise today, do the same tomorrow, and over time dramatic results may occur.

Possessing the power to change ourselves minimizes the fear of being ruled by appetites. For, as Epicurus observes, "that which is in our control is subject to no master."[9] In other words, if we can learn to control our desires, then we need not fear their controlling us.

20

FEAR OF DEATH

Death looms for all. Like boaters riding a long rapids flowing inexorably toward a deadly waterfall, we can take pleasure in the passing scene so long as we do not focus on where we are headed. What we cannot do, however, is stop the current or change its direction. We are caught in the grip of time.

This picture, which we find compelling, is one Epicurus wishes to deny. In his view, if we focus on death and fear it, then we are led to be unhappy and cannot enjoy our lives.

His counterargument is straightforward. Death should be of no concern to the living or the dead, because those who are living are not dead and those who are dead don't exist. As he puts it, "death, the most terrifying of ills, is nothing to us, since so long as we exist, death is not with us; but when death comes, then we do not exist."[1]

For Epicurus, therefore, death should not affect the enjoyment of life. Rather, death is simply the cessation of living. And what is dreadful about not being alive?

Perhaps the best-known argument for this conclusion was developed by the Roman poet and philosopher Lucretius, who lived in the first half of the century before the birth of Jesus. Lucretius wrote the epic poem *De rerum natura* (On the nature of things), in which he expounds the philosophy of Epicurus. On the subject of death Lucretius argues that just as we are unconcerned whether we had lived at any time before we were born, so we should be equally unconcerned whether we live at any time after we die. As he says, "Look back now and consider how the bygone ages of eternity that elapsed before our birth were nothing to us. Here, then, is a mirror in which nature shows us the time to come after our death. Do you see anything fearful in it? Do you perceive anything grim? Does it not appear more peaceful than the deepest sleep?"[2]

This puzzle about the asymmetry of our views of life before birth and after death has been much discussed by contemporary philosophers.[3] Thomas Nagel contends that the option of a person's living earlier than the time of birth isn't possible, because a person born earlier wouldn't be the same person. Shelly Kagan replies that Nagel's claim is mistaken because a situation can be imagined in which a person born earlier would be the same person as the one born later. For example, a fertility clinic could have sperm and eggs available and decide when to bring them together. Once that union is formed, a person is soon born, and Kagan maintains that because the union could have been formed earlier, the resultant person could have been born earlier.

Regardless of how that metaphysical disagreement is resolved, one asymmetry between past and future remains. We know more or less what happened in the past but not what will happen in the future. Thus most of us have less curiosity about events in the past than about events in the future. Hence life after death is of much greater interest than life before birth.

Consider this analogous situation. You and your friend arrive at a baseball game in the third inning. Unfortunately after the sixth inning you have to leave. When you express disappointment at not being able to stay longer, your friend responds, "You're not much interested now in seeing a tape of innings that occurred before we arrived. Why are you concerned to see innings that will occur after we leave?" The obvious answer is that we want to know the score at a time after we leave; we already know the score at any time before we arrived.

Kagan concludes that "what's bad about death is that when you're dead, you're not experiencing the good things in life."[4] Epicurus's reply would be that because "all good and evil consists in sensation" and "death is deprivation of sensation," then "there is nothing terrible in not living."[5]

On this matter we agree with Kagan and Nagel, both of whom view death as an evil, because, in Nagel's words, "death, no matter how inevitable, is an abrupt cancellation of indefinitely extensive possible goods."[6] Thus, other things being equal, the longer you live well, the better. Yet even if Epicurus is correct that death is not bad for the person who dies, it may be catastrophic for others, who may be immeasurably worse off, deprived of the presence of someone whose life was of inestimable value.

Here we arrive at an internal difficulty in the thought of Epicurus. As he says, "Of all the things which wisdom acquires to produce the blessedness of the complete life, far the greatest is the possession of friendship."[7] Yet death can take away a friend, thereby causing despondency. The closer the friendship, the greater the despair. Therefore we do have reason to fear death—perhaps not our own but the death of those we love. When Epicurus concludes that "there is nothing terrible in not living," he is thinking only of the one who is dead, not of those still alive.

Indeed, the sequence of deaths is a matter of import. For instance, two friends may in one respect be better off dying together, for both are saved the pain of living without the other.

The situation is reminiscent of the Zen story titled "Real Prosperity."

A rich man asked Sengai to write something for the continued prosperity of his family, so that it might be treasured from generation to generation.

Sengai obtained a large sheet of paper and wrote: "Father dies, son dies, grandson dies."

The rich man became angry. "I asked you to write something for the happiness of my family. Why do you make such a joke as this?"

"No joke is intended," explained Sengai. "If before you yourself die your son should die, this would grieve you greatly. If your grandson should pass away before your son, both of you would be brokenhearted. If your family, generation after generation, passes away in the order I have named, it will be the natural course of life. I call this real prosperity."[8]

In brief, regardless of whatever *my* death may mean to me, *your* death may mean everything.

In concluding our discussion of Epicurus, we should emphasize that he offers numerous practical insights about finding satisfaction in the human condition. In particular, he rightfully reminds us not to be filled with desire for goods others may have while failing to appreciate the goods we ourselves possess: "Nothing satisfies the man who is not satisfied with a little."[9]

Nevertheless, we do not share his outlook entirely, particularly his dismissal of death as irrelevant to the concerns of the living. In fact, our viewpoint is better captured by a work with some similar themes written by someone not in the Hellenistic tradition but in the Hebraic tradition, someone whose identity is unknown but whose description of the world and our place in it is profound. The text we refer to is found in the Bible, in the book known in Hebrew as *Koheleth* and in English as "Ecclesiastes."

21

FUTILITY

The Bible attributes the Book of Ecclesiastes to Koheleth, traditionally identified with Solomon, son of David and Bathsheba, powerful king of Israel, builder of the Temple in Jerusalem, famed for his wealth and wisdom. While modern scholarship does not accept the ascription of the Book to Solomon,[1] Koheleth is presented as one who possesses riches, authority, and prestige.

The dating of Ecclesiastes is uncertain, but several leading authorities believe it to be a work of the fourth or third centuries B.C.E., that is, about the time of Epicurus or somewhat later.[2] Given the interaction between the Hebrew and Greek cultures that occurred during this period, certain common themes might have influenced both Epicurus and the author of Ecclesiastes, although the matter remains murky. In any case, some similarities in outlook between the two are striking, although rarely noted.

Koheleth, of course, is a monotheist, whereas Epicurus is a polytheist, but in neither case is the divine the center of attention. As we have previously discussed, Epicurus affirms that the gods exist but denies that they have any effect on human events. Koheleth refers to God only occasionally and not in standard ways. As Robert Alter writes, "[Koheleth] has enough of a connection with tradition that he never absolutely denies the idea of a personal god, but his [God] often seems to be a stand-in for the cosmic powers-that-be, for fate or the overarching dynamic of reality that is beyond human control."[3] God may eventually judge us, but when, how, or by what standards is unclear. After all, "sometimes a good man perishes in spite of his goodness, and sometimes a wicked one endures in spite of his wickedness."[4] No afterlife is anticipated in which such injustices are corrected.

Both outlooks maintain that the pattern of world events is cyclical. Epicurus notes: "Nothing new happens in the universe, if you consider the infinite time past."[5] Koheleth famously remarks:

> Only that shall happen
> Which has happened.
> Only that occur
> Which has occurred;
> There is nothing new
> Beneath the sun!ature[6]

Epicurus seeks tranquility by living what Tim O'Keefe describes as "a moderately ascetic life."[7] In a memorable poem Koheleth also urges moderation:

> A season is set for everything, a time for every experience under
>   heaven;
> A time for being born and a time for dying,
> A time for planting and a time for uprooting the planted;
> A time for slaying and a time for healing,
> A time for tearing down and a time for building up;
> A time for weeping and a time for laughing,
> A time for wailing and a time for dancing;
> A time for throwing stones and a time for gathering stones,[8]
> A time for embracing and a time for shunning embraces;

A time for seeking and a time for losing,
A time for keeping and a time for discarding;
A time for ripping and a time for sewing,
A time for silence and a time for speaking;
A time for loving and a time for hating;
A time for war and a time for peace.[9]

The natural order has a balance that should be respected. In particular, no aspect of life should be pursued so single-mindedly as to blot out concern for other activities.

Like Epicurus, Koheleth especially disparages riches and fame: "Then my thoughts turned to all the fortune my hands had built up, to the wealth I had acquired and won—and oh, it was all futile and pursuit of wind; there was no real value under the sun."[10] As to renown, Koheleth warns that "the wise man, just like the fool, is not remembered forever; for, as the succeeding days roll by, both are forgotten."[11]

Not only is the quest for money and renown futile, so is every other pursuit.

"Utter futility!—said Koheleth—
Utter futility! All is futile!"[12]

The Hebrew word is "hevel" (rhymes with "level"), which can be translated as "futility," "vanity," "absurdity," "nothingness," or "mere breath." Regardless, the point is that all efforts are ultimately useless. We may have high hopes for success over the long run, but as John Maynard Keynes put it bluntly, "*In the long run* we are all dead."[13]

Here we arrive at a major difference between Epicurus and Koheleth. Epicurus finds hope for humanity in exercising reason and acting with restraint. Koheleth, while not denying value to wisdom and thoughtful behavior, views any strategy we may adopt as mere temporizing in the face of approaching doom. As regards death, man is akin to the beasts: "Both go to the same place; both came from dust and both return to dust."[14]

Epicurus argues that once we understand death, we can be unconcerned about it and continue to find value in our existence. Koheleth disagrees, maintaining that once we understand death, we should recognize how much of our strivings it renders pointless. "So, too, I loathed all the wealth that I was gaining under the sun. For I shall leave it to the man who will succeed me—and who knows whether he will be wise or foolish?—and he will control all the wealth that I gained by toil and wisdom under the sun. That too is futile."[15] As Michael V. Fox comments, "What really distresses Koheleth is not the loss of his wealth but the inconsequentiality of his labors."[16]

A related difference between Epicurus and Koheleth concerns the place of chance in human events. Epicurus recognizes it as having a role but a relatively minor one. "In yet few things chance hinders a wise man, but the greatest and most important matters reason has ordained and throughout the whole period of life does and will ordain."[17] For Koheleth, on the contrary:

> I have further observed under the sun that
> The race is not won by the swift,
> Nor the battle by the valiant;
> Nor is bread won by the wise,
> Nor wealth by the intelligent,
> Nor favor by the learned.
> For the time of mischance comes to all.[18]

Given that Koheleth views death as undermining much of our efforts in life and recognizes that death can come at any time without warning, he affords chance a much larger role than does Epicurus, to whom death is nothing.

Surprisingly, although Epicurus and Koheleth hold different views of death and chance, they advocate quite similar approaches to living well. We turn to these next.

22

LIVING WELL

Both Epicurus and Koheleth urge acting ethically. Epicurus understands justice to be "a pledge of mutual advantage to restrain men from harming one another and save them from being harmed." Keeping this pledge is in the interest of all: "It is hard for an evil-doer to escape detection, but to obtain security for escaping is impossible." Furthermore, "a man who causes fear cannot be free from fear."[1] Thus the moral path is always wisest.

Koheleth likewise notes the foolishness of immorality. "Cheating may rob the wise man of reason and destroy the prudence of the cautious."[2] Also, "it will not be well with the scoundrel."[3] Throughout the centuries commentators have wondered how Koheleth reconciles this observation with recognizing that "sometimes a wicked one endures in spite of his wickedness."[4] Perhaps Koheleth is admitting that the wicked one may endure for a while but eventually is likely to be undone by excess,[5] a point also made by Epicurus.

Apart from being moral, however, what is involved in living well? For Epicurus, as we have seen, the answer is found in seeking pleasure, remembering that the worthiness of each pleasure must be judged in terms of whatever pains it may bring.

Incidentally, that caution was offered in an especially charming manner two millennia later by Benjamin Franklin.[6] He tells the story of how, when he was seven years old, he spent all his money in a toy shop to buy a whistle, which over time gave him less pleasure than he had anticipated. Later in life he observed many people overestimating the value of things they sought, making too great sacrifices to obtain, for example, fine clothes, fine houses, fine furniture, wealth, popularity, or what Franklin called "mere corporeal Sensations." He said of those who made such unwise choices that they had paid too much for their whistle. This warning captures the spirit of Epicurus.

As for Koheleth, he offers a single formula for living well and repeats it often: "There is nothing worthwhile for a man but to eat and drink and afford himself enjoyment with his means."[7] Again: "Only this, I have found, is a real good: that one should eat and drink and get pleasure with all the gains he makes under the sun, during the numbered days of life that God has given him; for that is his portion."[8] Yet again: "I therefore praised enjoyment. For the only good a man can have under the sun is to eat and drink and enjoy himself."[9] Finally, "Go, eat your bread in gladness, and drink your wine in joy; for your action was long ago approved by God. Let your clothes be freshly washed, and your head never lack ointment. Enjoy happiness with a woman you love all the fleeting days of your life that have been granted to you under the sun—all your fleeting days. For that alone is what you can get out of life and out of the means you acquire under the sun."[10]

The message is clear: enjoy yourself pursuing whatever activities in which you find delight. Only two conditions need to be remembered. First, always act morally. Second, be prudent. As Koheleth advises, "he who digs a pit will fall into it."[11]

Are any particular activities recommended by Epicurus or Koheleth? Both praise friendship. Epicurus writes that "of all the things which wisdom acquires to produce the blessedness of the complete life, far the greatest is the possession of friendship."[12] Koheleth similarly remarks that "two are better off than one, in that they have greater benefit from their earnings. For should they fall, one can raise the other; but woe betide him who is alone and falls with no companion to raise him!"[13] For neither Epicurus and Koheleth is friendship a requirement, but both strongly recommend it.

One intriguing difference between them regards sexual activity. Epicurus comments: "You tell me that the stimulus of the flesh makes you too prone to the pleasures of love. Provided that you do not break the laws or good customs and do not distress any of your neighbors or do harm to your body or squander your pittance, you may indulge your inclination as you please. Yet it is impossible not to come up against one or other of these barriers; for the pleasures of love never profited a man and he is lucky if they do him no harm." Furthermore: "Sexual intercourse has never done a man good, and he is lucky if it has not harmed him."[14]

Koheleth takes a wholly different approach. Recall his recognizing "a time for embracing and a time for shunning embraces" as well as "a time for loving and a time for hating."[15] And also this advice: "Enjoy happiness with a woman you love all the fleeting days of life that have been granted to you under the sun—all your fleeting days."[16] After all, Solomon is said to have had seven hundred royal wives and three hundred concubines, and his father, King David, was hardly a model of asceticism.[17]

Note that Judaism has traditionally been unequivocally in favor of marriage and of passionate sex within marriage. Such is not the case with Christianity. For instance, St. Paul says: "It is well for a man not to touch a woman," and "I wish that all were as I myself am," that is, unmarried.[18] Even apart from St. Paul's metaphysical view that "nothing good dwells within me, that is, in my flesh,"[19] he offers this argument against marriage: "The unmarried man is anxious about the affairs of the Lord, but the married man is anxious about the affairs of the world, how to please his wife, and his interests are divided. And the unmarried woman and the virgin are anxious about the affairs of the Lord, so that they may be holy in body and spirit, but the married woman is anxious about the affairs of the world, how to please her husband."[20]

The celibacy of priests and nuns thus has biblical support. Rabbis, however, are expected to marry, because Judaism considers marriage an essential human relationship, bringing joy to both partners. Sex is not a "concession"[21] but an embodiment of the human capacity for love.

Neither Epicurus nor Koheleth offers any extended list of worthwhile activities. Both urge the seeking of pleasure, although Epicurus understands it as tranquility, a cautious choice, while Koheleth prefers enjoyment, a less abstemious option. But either approach, pursued ethically, can bring satisfaction, the prescription for living well.

SATISFACTION

Satisfied people are content with their lot. They have a favorable impression of their lives and do not suffer excessively from anxiety, alienation, frustration, disappointment, or depression. They may face problems but overall see more positives than negatives.

The crucial point is that how one achieves satisfaction differs from person to person. One individual may be satisfied only by earning ten million dollars. Another may be satisfied by going every day with friends to a favorite club to swim, eat lunch, and play cards. Another may be satisfied by acting in community theater productions. One path is as good as another so long as contentment is found.

We are reminded of the true story of the young man who was complaining that he couldn't find an appropriate woman to marry. When asked whether any of his friends had been more fortunate, he replied with a touch of disdain that one had married recently but that the woman he had married was not pretty. Someone listening to the conversation then asked, "Does your friend find this woman attractive?" The young man replied, "Yes, very much so." To which the questioner responded, "That's all that matters. What you think is of no account."

Some may be poor, yet satisfied. Others may be alone, yet satisfied. Still others may find satisfaction regardless of the depth of their learning or self-knowledge and irrespective of whatever illness or disability they may face. In any case, the judgment of satisfaction is the individual's, not anyone else's.

Does satisfaction depend on achieving one's goals? Not necessarily. You may achieve your aims only to find that doing so does not provide the satisfaction for which you had hoped. For example, you might eagerly seek and gain admission to a prestigious college only to find that its rural location, which seemed an advantage when you applied, turns out to be a disadvantage when you develop interests better pursued in an urban environment.

Furthermore, some people don't have specific goals. They can happily live here or there, engage in a wide variety of hobbies, or even pursue various careers. They find delight in spontaneity. Perhaps that approach to life doesn't appeal to you, but so what? If it works for others, why not let them have their enjoyment without derogating it?

How fortunate that not everyone seeks satisfaction in the same ways. Suppose everyone wanted to become a lawyer, live in Vermont, or vacation at the same beach. Fortunately, such is not the case.

Finding satisfaction is not easy. Consider Hume's account of the sixteenth-century emperor Charles V of Spain, who "tired with human grandeur . . . resigned all his extensive dominions into the hands of his son. In the last harangue which he made on that memorable occasion, he publicly avowed, *that the greatest prosperities that he had ever enjoyed, had been mixed with so many adversities, that he might truly say he had never enjoyed any satisfaction or contentment.*"[1]

In case you might suppose that a life with intellectual accomplishment would be more satisfactory, consider Hume's account of Cicero, whose "fortune, from small beginnings, rose to the greatest luster and renown; yet what pathetic complaints of the ills of life do his familiar letters, as well as philosophical discourses, contain?"[2]

How do you achieve satisfaction, considering that it has eluded so many, including powerful kings and eminent thinkers? Both Epicurus and Koheleth offer similar suggestions. They agree that the key to satisfaction lies within yourself, because you cannot control the events outside you. If your satisfaction depends on whether others praise you, then they control how satisfied you will be with your life. If you wish to avoid being subject to the power of others, then you have to free yourself from dependence on their judgments.

Perhaps some, such as Philippa Foot, will be unimpressed when they "look back on the life of a man or woman who has in fact spent a lifetime in childish pursuits."[3] Who is to say, however, which pursuits are "childish"? How about collecting dolls, telling jokes, planting vegetables, selling cookies, running races, recounting adventures, or singing songs? While children engage in all these activities, so do adults, who may thereby find satisfaction in their lives. Why disparage them or their interests?

An activity that one individual believes fatuous may satisfy another. Metaphysical inquiry, for instance, is engrossing for some, but to a tough-minded business executive may seem a waste of time, providing no insight into acquiring wealth or influence. A philosopher of art may wish to develop an aesthetic analysis of Francis Ford Coppola's *The Godfather,* whereas a historian of the film industry may be far more interested in learning the story of the struggles behind the movie's production, including the extraordinary means by which powerful attorney Sidney Korshak arranged for Al Pacino, who was under contract to MGM, to star in a production by rival Paramount.[4] Some may not even want to know such sordid details, while others will relish them. Both, however, can find satisfaction in pursuing their respective interests.

Obituaries provide information about people's lives, detailing their accomplishments. What we don't learn therein, however, is whether a particular person's life brought satisfaction. Granted contentment and success may sometimes go together, but, given the choice, would you rather die unhappy with many credits, or happy without much acclaim? Both Epicurus and Koheleth make the case for choosing the latter option. We find their outlook sagacious.

24

CONCLUDING QUESTIONS

Let us now return to the two fictional cases with which our discussion began: Pat and Lee. Pat, you may recall, is a successful philosopher who is happily married and enjoys playing bridge and the cello. Lee did not attend college, is single and financially independent, makes philanthropic gifts, and enjoys sunbathing, swimming, and surfing, along with freely spending money on a variety of luxurious items, including homes, cars, and golfing holidays. Both treat others with respect and are satisfied with their lives.

Here are the questions we asked about Pat and Lee: Are both living well? Are both pursuing equally successful lives? Is either life wasted? We can answer now that both are living well, both are finding equal success in living, and the life of neither is wasted. We might admire one more than the other, but such a judgment would reflect our own preferences or purposes and not serve as an appropriate basis for determining whose life is well-lived.

We recognize, however, that others may not agree with us. Hence we shall raise and respond to their most likely questions.

First, do we claim that Pat and Lee are contributing equally to the welfare of society? No. Pat's teaching, research, and service are unmatched by any activity of Lee, although Lee's contributing money for worthy causes should be applauded. Thus if the question to be answered is which of the two is a more valuable member of society, the probable answer is Pat. The question, however, is not whose life is more useful to others but whose life is going better, viewing happiness from the perspective of the person being assessed. Because both individuals are acting morally and finding satisfaction, both lives are going well.

Note, incidentally, that if importance to the life of the community were the criterion for living well, philosophers would rank below those who collect garbage, maintain piping for water, repair electrical equipment, make goods from raw materials, and grow and prepare food. Life will go on in the temporary absence of philosophers, but try to survive even a month without garbage workers, plumbers, electricians, and those who labor in factories, on farms, or in kitchens. Are their lives, therefore, better than those of philosophers? We don't believe so. Living well should not be judged in terms of meeting societal needs.

A second question: Are we claiming that Pat and Lee are equally successful in terms of professional accomplishments? Obviously not. Pat has a series of notable scholarly achievements and is highly regarded by philosophical colleagues. Lee has no such record. Living well, however, is not determined by the length of your vita. While you may be renowned in your discipline (although probably unknown to those in other fields), you may still be deeply distressed, perhaps resulting from unresolved personal problems or continued frustration that you are not as celebrated as you would prefer. In either case, even though successful in one respect, you are not living well.

Third, does our view imply that an individual who is living well has no reason to undertake new endeavors? Not at all. As we stated at the beginning of our inquiry, a person's life can be assessed in many ways, and nothing is amiss about valuing goals apart from living well. Thus Pat may undertake to write a new book, or Lee may plan to travel to a hitherto unvisited location. Pat may take up golf, while Lee may learn to play bridge. Indeed, either may grow weary of their present activities and embark on a new phase of life, perhaps involving greater effort or much less.

The essential point is implicit in a fable titled "The Bear and the Beaver," authored by philosopher Charles Frankel, who taught at Columbia University, served as assistant secretary of state for educational and cultural affairs, and later was a founder and first president of the National Humanities Center. A bear who spends most of his time on vacation or hibernating meets a beaver who is always working hard at building dams. Each agrees to try the life of the other. The bear begins collecting twigs, knitting them together with mud, and putting them on logs he drags with mighty effort into the middle of the stream. Meanwhile, the beaver naps and relaxes. Finally after months of exhausting effort the bear decides, "I think I'll go back and be a bear." The beaver then looks at the bear heading for the hills and calls after him, "If you don't mind, I think I'll go back and be a bear too."[1]

Whether one decides, in essence, to be a beaver like Pat or a bear like Lee is a personal choice. After all, a life devoted to simple pursuits may yield as much satisfaction as one given to complex undertakings. That insight doesn't imply that arduous tasks are to be avoided, only that those who engage in them may not live better than those who don't. After all, if success in the most demanding intellectual activities were necessary for living well, then how many individuals would have lived as well as Aristotle, da Vinci, Shakespeare, Bach, Newton, or Einstein? Yet while their achievements were monumental, matching their incredible output is not necessary for living well. Few have thought as profoundly as they, but many have lived at least as ethically and contentedly.

In any case, you can live well while striving to fulfill cherished ambitions, whatever they may be. The key to doing so is realizing that almost surely some will achieve more than you, while others will achieve less. If you can be satisfied with whatever you accomplish, you can attain happiness.

A fourth and final question is whether we are suggesting that living well should be everyone's aim. Such is not our view. Dr. Martin Luther King Jr., for example, had an enormous impact on his own and future generations. Had he been deeply dissatisfied with his life, as we believe is contrary to fact, then he would have been putting the welfare of others ahead of his own interest, sacrificing the opportunity for personal contentment to benefit others. In that case, we would all be deeply grateful for his actions while recognizing the price he had to pay.

But wasn't his life good? The question is ambiguous. If "good" means consequential or praiseworthy, then his life surely was good. If, however, "good" implies being satisfied, then had he been dispirited and dismayed by his life, it would not have been good for him, although it would have benefitted countless others.

The question arises whether we should think primarily of our own welfare and that of our loved ones or instead be willing to sacrifice our well-being for the good of others who may be unknown to us. The soldier who jumps on a live grenade and thereby saves comrades dies valiantly but relinquishes the opportunity to continue living. Such an action is supererogatory, that is, beyond the call of duty, and, while highly commendable, neither required nor expected.

In sum, living well is up to you, because your happiness is within your power, as is the decision whether to act morally. Granted, infrequently the two conditions might pull in opposing directions. In particular, a supererogatory action, serving others, could lead to neglecting your own happiness, or, on the contrary, a violation of an ethical guideline, neglecting others, could lead to serving your own happiness. In either situation, forced to make what may be a wrenching decision, you would be, as Jean-Paul Sartre writes, "alone, with no excuses."[2]

Fortunately such conflicts are rare. Usually living well is sensible, admirable, and preferable. Hence we conclude by echoing what we understand to be Koheleth's advice, as astute today as when offered more than two thousand years ago: Be good and enjoy.

NOTES

2. WASTED LIVES?

1. Ronald Dworkin, *Religion Without God* (Cambridge, Mass.: Harvard University Press, 2013), 2, 11.
2. Ibid., 2, 10, 43, 46, 59.
3. Ibid., 114, 155.
4. Ibid., 157–58.
5. Ibid., 158.
6. Richard Taylor, *Good and Evil: A New Direction* (London: Macmillan, 1970), 259.
7. Harry Frankfurt, "Reply to Susan Wolf," in *Contours of Agency: Essays on Themes from Harry Frankfurt*, eds. Sarah Buss and Lee Overton (Cambridge, Mass.: MIT Press, 2002), 250.
8. See, for example, Stephen Darwall, *Welfare and Rational Care* (Princeton, N.J.: Princeton University Press, 2002); Richard Kraut, *What Is Good and Why* (Cambridge, Mass.: Harvard University Press, 2007); Susan Wolf, "Happiness and Meaning: Two Aspects of the Good Life," *Social Philosophy and Policy* 14, no. 1 (1997), and *Meaning in Life and Why It Matters: The Ethics of Well-Being* (Princeton, N.J.: Princeton University Press, 2010).

3. PROJECTS OF WORTH?

1. Wolf, "Happiness and Meaning," 209; *Meaning in Life*, 14, 37.
2. Wolf, "Happiness and Meaning," 209.

3. Wolf, "Happiness and Meaning," 209, 210; *Meaning in Life*, 14, 16, 24, 37.
4. Wolf, "Happiness and Meaning," 210, 211; *Meaning in Life*, 14, 15, 16, 24.
5. Wolf, "Happiness and Meaning," 211.
6. Wolf, *Meaning in Life*, 11, 21.
7. Wolf, "Happiness and Meaning," 217.
8. Ibid., 210.
9. Ibid.
10. Wolf, *Meaning in Life*, 27, 124.
11. Ibid., 124.
12. Ibid., 8.
13. Jonathan Haidt, "Comment," in *Meaning in Life*, 95, 97.
14. Wolf, *Meaning in Life*, 131.
15. Ibid., 3, 124, 130.

4. FLOURISHING?

1. Kraut, *What Is Good and Why*, 137, 131.
2. Sidney Hook, *Education for Modern Man: A New Perspective* (New York: Knopf, 1963), 69.
3. Kraut, *What Is Good and Why*, 147, 191.
4. See his *Method of Modern Jazz Piano Playing*, rev. ed. (Boston: Boston Music Company, 1937).
5. Known as Camp Encore/Coda, it continues under the directorship of Phil Saltman's son and daughter-in-law; its history can be found at www .encore-coda.com.
6. Kraut, *What Is Good and Why*, 45, 50, 79, 143–44, 146, 162, 165, 171.
7. Ibid., 123, 142–43, 169, 178, 183, 187.
8. Ibid., 178.
9. Ibid., 143, 167.
10. Ibid., 164.

5. THINGS THAT MATTER?

1. Darwall, *Welfare and Rational Care*, 75, 78.
2. *The Middle Works of John Dewey, 1899–1924*, vol. 9, *Democracy and Education*, ed. Jo Ann Boydston (Carbondale: Southern Illinois University Press, 1985), 247.
3. Darwall, *Welfare and Rational Care*, 95, 98.
4. Ibid., 79.

5. The story is related in her John Dewey Lecture, "How It Was," reprinted in *Portraits of American Philosophy*, ed. Steven M. Cahn (Lanham, Md.: Rowman & Littlefield, 2013), 47–61.

6. Darwall, *Welfare and Rational Care*, 76.

7. Ibid., 77–78.

8. Ibid., 79.

9. John Manley Robinson, *An Introduction to Early Greek Philosophy* (Boston: Houghton Mifflin Company, 1968), 52.

10. The *locus classicus* is Book X of the *Nicomachean Ethics*, trans. David Ross, rev. J. L. Ackrill and J. O. Urmson (Oxford: Oxford University Press, 1998), where at 1178a5 Aristotle maintains that a life of contemplation is "best and pleasantest."

11. Neil Levy, "Downshifting and Meaning in Life," *Ratio* 18, no. 2 (2005), 187, 188.

6. MORALITY AND HAPPINESS

1. Frankfurt, "Reply to Susan Wolf," 247.

2. Philippa Foot, *Moral Dilemmas* (Oxford: Clarendon Press, 2002), 35.

3. Matthew Cashen and Larry May, "The Happy Immoralist: Reply to Cahn," *Journal of Social Philosophy* 35, no. 1 (2004), 16.

4. Jeffrie G. Murphy, "The Unhappy Immoralist," *Journal of Social Philosophy* 35, no. 1 (2004), 11.

5. Ibid., 12.

6. John Kleinig, "Happiness and Virtue," *Journal of Social Philosophy* 35, no. 1 (2004), 2.

7. Lewis Carroll, *Through the Looking-Glass and What Alice Found There*, in *Alice in Wonderland*, ed. Donald J. Gray (New York: Norton, 1971), 163.

7. MORALITY AND UNHAPPINESS

1. Cashen and May, "The Happy Immoralist," 17.

2. Kleinig, "Happiness and Virtue," 2.

3. Diana Tietjens Meyers, "The Three Freds and the Fate of Their Happiness," *Journal of Social Philosophy* 35, no. 1 (2004), 9.

8. CHARACTER

1. Christopher W. Gowans, "Should Fred Elicit Our Derision or Our Compassion?", *Journal of Social Philosophy* 35, no. 1 (2004), 14.

2. Bernard Gert, "Comments on Cahn's 'The Happy Immoralist,'" *Journal of Social Philosophy* 35, no. 1 (2004), 19.

9. APPEARING MORAL

1. Michael Argyle, "Causes and Correlates of Happiness," in *Well-Being: The Foundations of Hedonic Psychology*, eds. Daniel Kahneman, Ed Diener, and Norbert Schwarz (New York: Russell Sage Foundation, 2003), 362.
2. Jean-Paul Sartre, *Existentialism Is a Humanism*, trans. Carol Macomber (New Haven: Yale University Press, 2007), 29.

11. HEAVEN AND HELL

1. See Blaise Pascal, *Pensees and Other Writings*, trans. Honor Levi (New York: Oxford University Press, 1995), 152–56.
2. Marc Scott Zucree, *The Twilight Zone Companion* (New York: Bantam Books, 1982), 242–44.

12. MORAL JUDGMENTS

1. Thomas Reid, *Essays on the Active Powers of the Human Mind* (Cambridge, Mass.: M.I.T. Press, 1969), 237.
2. Jonathan Harrison, "Empiricism in Ethics," *Philosophical Quarterly* 2, no. 9 (1952), 306.
3. James Rachels, "Egoism and Moral Scepticism," in *A New Introduction to Philosophy*, ed. Steven M. Cahn (New York: Harper & Row, 1971), 432–33.
4. P. H. Nowell-Smith, *Ethics* (Baltimore: Penguin Books, 1954), 142–43.
5. David Hume, *An Enquiry Concerning the Principles of Morals* (New York: Liberal Arts Press, 1957), 103.
6. *The Maxims of La Rochefoucauld*, trans. Louis Kronenberger (New York: Random House, 1959), #379.

13. MORAL STANDARDS

1. Matthew 7:12, *The Holy Bible: New Revised Standard Version* (New York and Oxford: Oxford University Press, 1989).
2. Shabbath, 31a, *The Babylonian Talmud* (London: Soncino Press, 1938).
3. Walter Kaufman, *The Faith of a Heretic* (New York: Doubleday, 1963), 212.
4. Immanuel Kant, *Foundations of the Metaphysics of Morals*, 2nd ed., trans. Lewis White Beck (Saddle River, N.J.: Prentice-Hall, 1997), 38–39.

5. John Stuart Mill, *Utilitarianism* (Indianapolis: Hackett, 1979), 10.

6. Kant, *Foundations of the Metaphysics of Morals*, 46.

14. CHOOSING THE EXPERIENCE MACHINE

1. Robert Nozick, *Anarchy, State, and Utopia* (New York: Basic Books, 1974), 42–43.

2. Matthew Silverstein, "In Defense of Happiness: A Response to the Experience Machine," *Social Theory and Practice* 26, no. 2 (2000), 281–82.

3. Jonathan Glover recognizes that the experience machine could be considered "an improved version of the cinema," and for that reason admits that he would try the machine "for brief periods" (*What Sort of People Should There Be?* [New York: Penguin Books, 1984], 92). But after doubting that most people would choose to plug in for extensive periods, if not the rest of their lives (thus suggesting that some might make such a choice), he goes awry by arguing against plugging in being made compulsory, a suggestion neither Nozick nor anyone else has proposed.

   Thomas Hurka also recognizes that "we use TV and movies as substitute experience machines" (*The Best Things in Life: A Guide to What Really Matters* [New York: Oxford University Press, 2011], 69). Yet he maintains that "for many of us a whole life of good feeling would lack important human goods." As for those who might not share his desire for hardships, he has no comment.

4. Nozick, *Anarchy, State, and Utopia*, 44.

5. Torbjorn Tannsjo cites the widespread use of drugs as the support for his contention that Nozick's argument is "in an almost obvious way, unsound" ("Narrow Hedonism," *Journal of Happiness Studies* 8, no. 1 [2007], 93–94). No other published work of which we are aware reaches the same conclusion.

6. Robert Nozick, *The Examined Life: Philosophical Meditations* (New York: Simon and Schuster, 1989), 105.

7. For an insightful assessment of the script, see Victor L. Cahn, *Walking Distance: Remembering Classic Episodes from Classic Television* (Eugene, Ore.: Wipf and Stock, 2014), 5–23.

8. Zucree, *The Twilight Zone Companion*, 42.

9. Nozick, *The Examined Life*, 105.

10. William Blake, *Auguries of Innocence*, lines 119–24.

11. Arthur Schopenhauer, *The World As Will And Representation*, trans. E. F. J. Payne, vol. 2 (New York: Dover, 1966), 573–74.

12. Nozick, *Anarchy, State, and Utopia*, 45.

13. Glover, *What Sort of People Should There Be?*, 285.
14. James Griffin, *Well-Being* (Oxford: Clarendon Press, 1986), 9.
15. L. W. Sumner, *Welfare, Happiness, and Ethics* (Oxford: Clarendon Press, 1999), 96.
16. David Hume, *Dialogues Concerning Natural Religion and Other Writings* (New York: Cambridge University Press, 2007), 69–70.

15. HAPPINESS AND IGNORANCE

1. Those interested in such issues may see Steven M. Cahn, *Saints and Scamps: Ethics in Academia*, 25th anniversary edition (Lanham, Md.: Rowman & Littlefield, 2011).
2. Richard Kraut, "Two Conceptions of Happiness," *Philosophical Review* 88, no. 2 (1979), 179.
3. Edwin Arlington Robinson, "Richard Cory," *Robinson: Poems*, ed. Scott Donaldson (New York: Knopf, 2007), 33.

16. ASSESSING ACHIEVEMENT

1. Julia Annas, *The Morality of Happiness* (New York: Oxford University Press, 1993), 349–50.
2. Epicurus, "Principal Doctrines," in *The Stoic and Epicurean Philosophers*, ed. Whitney J. Oates, trans. C. Bailey (New York: Random House, 1940), 36.

17. PLEASURES AND PAINS

1. Epicurus, "Letter to Menoeceus," in *The Stoic and Epicurean Philosophers*, ed. Whitney J. Oates, trans. C. Bailey (New York: Random House, 1940), 32.
2. Epicurus, "Fragments" in *The Stoic and Epicurean Philosophers*, ed. Whitney J. Oates, trans. C. Bailey (New York: Random House, 1940), 44.
3. Alfred North Whitehead, *The Aims of Education and Other Essays* (New York: The Free Press, 1929), 34.
4. Epicurus, "Letter to Menoeceus," 32.

18. FEAR OF THE DIVINE

1. Epicurus, "Letter to Menoeceus," 30.
2. Mortimer J. Cohen, *Pathways Through the Bible* (Philadelphia: Jewish Publication Society of America, 1946), 460.

3. Jack J. Cohen, *The Case for Religious Naturalism* (New York: Reconstructionist Press, 1958), 83.
4. Hume, *Dialogues Concerning Natural Religion*, 74.
5. Ibid., 101–2.
6. Epicurus, "Letter to Menoeceus," 30.
7. We take the term from Lewis Carroll's humorous poem, "The Hunting of the Snark: An Agony in Eight Fits." It concludes: "For the Snark was a Boojum, you see," thus explaining one unknown concept in terms of another and leaving both without sense. See the complete text in *Alice in Wonderland*, 213–30.
8. *Xunzi: Basic Writings*, trans. Burton Watson (New York: Columbia University Press, 2003), 89.
9. "Introduction," *The Epicurus Reader: Selected Writings and Testimonia*, eds. and trans. Brad Inwood and L. P. Gerson (Indianapolis: Hackett, 1994), ix.

19. FEAR OF UNFULFILLED DESIRES

1. Epicurus, "Principal Doctrines," 37.
2. Ibid., 36.
3. Ibid.
4. Gordon S. Wood, *Empire of Liberty: A History of the Early Republic, 1789–1815* (New York: Oxford University Press, 2009), 206.
5. *The Republic of Plato*, trans. Francis MacDonald Cornford (New York: Oxford University Press, 1945), 620d.
6. Epicurus, "Fragments," 47.
7. Dewey, *Democracy and Education*, 136.
8. Aristotle, *Nicomachean Ethics*, Book X, 1117b25.
9. Epicurus, "Letter to Menoeceus," 33.

20. FEAR OF DEATH

1. Epicurus, "Letter to Menoeceus," 31.
2. Lucretius, *On the Nature of Things*, trans. Martin Ferguson Smith (Indianapolis: Hackett, 2001), 94.
3. See, for example, Thomas Nagel, "Death," in *Mortal Questions* (Cambridge, U.K.: Cambridge University Press, 1979), 1–10; Fred Feldman, *Conversations with the Reaper* (Oxford: Oxford University Press, 1992), 154–56; and Shelly Kagan, *Death* (New Haven: Yale University Press, 2012), 224–33.
4. Kagan, *Death*, 235
5. Epicurus, "Letter to Menoeceus," 30–31.

6. Nagel, "Death," 10.

7. Epicurus, "Principal Doctrines," 37.

8. *Zen Flesh/Zen Bones: A Collection of Zen and Pre-Zen Writings*, compiled by Paul Reps and Nyogen Senzaki (North Clarendon, Vt.: Tuttle, 1957), 89.

9. Epicurus, "Fragments," 51.

21. FUTILITY

1. Michael V. Fox, *The JPS Bible Commentary: Ecclesiastes* (Philadelphia: Jewish Publication Society, 2004), x. For our understanding of the text and its background, we are indebted to Fox's work as well as to insights offered by Robert Alter in his *The Wisdom Books: A Translation with Commentary* (New York: Norton, 2010).

2. Fox, *JPS Bible Commentary*, x; Alter, *Wisdom Books*, 338.

3. Alter, *Wisdom Books*, 341.

4. Ecclesiastes 7:15.

5. Epicurus, "Fragments," 50.

6. Ecclesiastes 1:9

7. Tim O'Keefe, *Epicureanism* (Berkeley: University of California Press, 2010), 107.

8. Possibly a reference to sexual activity.

9. Ecclesiastes 3:1–8.

10. Ecclesiastes 2:11.

11. Ecclesiastes 2:16.

12. Ecclesiastes 1:2.

13. John Maynard Keynes, *A Tract on Monetary Reform* (London: Macmillan, 1971), 65.

14. Ecclesiastes 3:20.

15. Ecclesiastes 2:18–19.

16. Fox, *JPS Bible Commentary*, 17.

17. Epicurus, "Principal Doctrines," 36.

18. Ecclesiastes 9:11.

22. LIVING WELL

1. Epicurus, "Principal Doctrines," 37; "Fragments," 40, 51.

2. Ecclesiastes 7:7.

3. Ecclesiastes 8:13.

4. Ecclesiastes 7:15.

5. Ecclesiastes 7:17.

6. Benjamin Franklin, *Franklin Writings*, ed. J. A. Leo Lemay (New York: Library of America, 1987), 931–33.
7. Ecclesiastes 2:24.
8. Ecclesiastes 5:17.
9. Ecclesiastes 8:15.
10. Ecclesiastes 9:7–9.
11. Ecclesiastes 10:8.
12. Epicurus, "Principal Doctrines," 37.
13. Ecclesiastes 4:9–10.
14. Epicurus, "Fragments," 42, 45.
15. Ecclesiastes 3:5, 3:8.
16. Ecclesiastes 9:9.
17. 1 Kings 11:3.
18. 1 Corinthians 7:1, 7:7.
19. Romans 7:18.
20. 1 Corinthians 7:33–34.
21. 1 Corinthians 7:6.

23. SATISFACTION

1. Hume, *Dialogues Concerning Natural Religion*, 73.
2. Ibid.
3. Philippa Foot, *Natural Goodness* (Oxford: Clarendon Press, 2001), 86.
4. For this astonishing story and numerous others about Sidney Korshak (1907–1996), who has been called "the most powerful lawyer in the world," see Gus Russo, *Supermob: How Sidney Korshak and His Criminal Associates Became America's Hidden Power Brokers* (New York: Bloomsbury, 2006).

24. CONCLUDING QUESTIONS

1. Charles Frankel, *The Love of Anxiety and Other Essays* (New York: Harper & Row, 1965), 95–104.
2. Jean-Paul Sartre, *Existentialism and Human Emotions* (New York: Kensington, 1957), 23.

INDEX

ABOUT THE AUTHORS

Steven M. Cahn is professor of philosophy at the Graduate Center of the City University of New York. He has written or edited some fifty books, including *Fate, Logic, and Time*; *God, Reason, and Religion*; *Saints and Scamps: Ethics in Academia*; and *From Student to Scholar: A Candid Guide to Becoming a Professor*.

* * *

Christine Vitrano is associate professor of philosophy at Brooklyn College, City University of New York. She is the author of *The Nature and Value of Happiness* and coeditor, with Steven M. Cahn, of *Happiness: Classic and Contemporary Readings in Philosophy*.